The Orchard Book
of **Funny Poems**

The Orchard Book of Nursery Rhymes

Faith Jaques

The Orchard Book of Nursery Stories

Sophie Windham

The Orchard Book of Fairy Tales

Retold by Rose Impey
Illustrated by Ian Beck

The Orchard Book of Greek Myths

Retold by Geraldine McCaughrean
Illustrated by Emma Chichester Clark

The Orchard Book of Magical Tales

Retold by Margaret Mayo
Illustrated by Jane Ray

The Orchard Book of Poems

Compiled by Adrian Mitchell

The Orchard Book
of Funny Poems

Compiled by

WENDY COPE

Illustrated by

AMANDA VESEY

ORCHARD BOOKS

For Pauline
A.V.

In memory of Margaret Arnold (1900 – 1991),
a good friend to every child she knew.

My thanks to the following for their advice and assistance: the staff of the
Saison Poetry Library, especially Dolores Conway, the children's librarian; Ian
Willison and John Barr of the British Library; Morag Styles.
Wendy Cope

First published in Great Britain in 1993 by
ORCHARD BOOKS
96 Leonard Street, London EC2A 4RH
Orchard Books Australia
14 Mars Road, Lane Cove, NSW 2066
Text © Wendy Cope 1993
Illustrations © Amanda Vesey 1993
The right of Wendy Cope to be identified as compiler of this work
and of Amanda Vesey as illustrator has been asserted by them in
accordance with the Copyright, Designs and Patents Act, 1988.
A CIP catalogue record for this book is available from the British Library.
1 85213 395 3
Printed in Singapore

Contents

Easy Money

Guess how old I am?
I bet you can't.
I bet you.
Go on guess.
Have a guess.

Wrong!
Have another.

Wrong!
Have another.

Wrong again!
Do you give in?

Seven years four months two weeks
five days three hours fifteen
minutes forty-eight seconds!
That's 20p you owe me.

Roger McGough

Telling

One, two, three, four,
Telling Miss that Gary swore.
Five, six, seven, eight,
Now I haven't got a mate.

Wendy Cope

A Quick Way of Counting to 100

1,2,
skip a few,
99, 100

Anon

1 × 2 is 2

1 × 2 is 2
2 × 2 are 4
3 × 2 are 9
4 × 2 are 17
5 × 2 are 26
6 × 2 are 39
7 × 2 are 148
8 × 2 are 2,204
9 × 2 are 330,916
10 × 2 are 999,999
11 × 2 are 5,222,506½
12 × 2 are 135,926,201

and if anyone says it isn't
meet me in the playground
tomorrow at high noon,
and don't be late! . . .

Paul Johnson

As I was Going to St Ives

As I was going to St Ives,
I met a man with seven wives;
Every wife had seven sacks;
Every sack had seven cats;
Every cat had seven kits.
Kits, cats, sacks, and wives –
How many were going to St Ives?

Anon

Answer: One. The others
were coming from St Ives.

ST. IVES

Three Riddled Riddles

1

I have nine legs.
I carry an umbrella.
I live in a box
at the bottom of a ship.
At night
I play the trombone.

What am I?

Answer: I've forgotten.

2

You see me at dawn
with the clouds in my hair.
I run like a horse
and sing like a nightingale.
I collect stamps
and coconuts.

What am I?

Answer: I'm not sure.

3

I taste like a grapefruit.
I swim like a chair.
I hang on the trees
and people tap my face,
rake my soil
and tell me jokes.

What am I?

Answer: I've really no idea.

Martyn Wiley and Ian McMillan

Cottleston Pie

Cottleston, Cottleston, Cottleston Pie,
A fly can't bird, but a bird can fly.
Ask me a riddle and I reply:
"Cottleston, Cottleston, Cottleston Pie."

Cottleston, Cottleston, Cottleston Pie,
A fish can't whistle and neither can I.
Ask me a riddle and I reply:
"Cottleston, Cottleston, Cottleston Pie."

Cottleston, Cottleston, Cottleston Pie,
Why does a chicken, I don't know why.
Ask me a riddle and I reply:
"Cottleston, Cottleston, Cottleston Pie."

A.A. Milne

Here Is the Nose that Smelled Something Sweet

Here is the Nose that smelled something sweet
And led the search for a bite to eat

Here are the Feet that followed the Nose
Around the kitchen on ten Tiptoes

Here are the Eyes that looked high and low
Till they spotted six pans sitting all in a row

Here are the Arms that reached up high
To bring down a fresh-baked blueberry pie

Here is the Mouth that opened up wide
Here are the Hands that put pie inside

Here is the Tongue that licked the tin
And lapped up the juice running down the Chin

Here is the Stomach that growled for more
Here are the Legs that ran for the door

Here are the Ears that heard a whack
Here is the Bottom that felt a smack!

Clyde Watson

14

If You're No Good at Cooking

If you're no good at cooking,
Can't fry or bake,

Here's something you
Can always make. Take

Three very ordinary
Slices of bread:

Stack the second
On the first one's head.

Stack the third
On top of that.

There! Your three slices
Lying pat.

So what have you got?
A BREAD SANDWICH,

That's what!
Why not?

Kit Wright

Christine Crump

Christine Crump is crunching crisps:
Cheese and onion, cheese and onion.
Christine Crump has crunched them.

Christine Crump is crunching crisps:
Smoky bacon, smoky bacon,
Cheese and onion, cheese and onion.
Christine Crump has crunched them.

Christine Crump is crunching crisps:
Ready salted, ready salted,
Smoky bacon, smoky bacon,
Cheese and onion, cheese and onion.
Christine Crump has crunched them.

Christine Crump is crunching crisps:
Curry flavour, curry flavour,
Ready salted, ready salted,
Smoky bacon, smoky bacon,
Cheese and onion, cheese and onion.
Christine Crump has crunched them.

Christine Crump is crunching crisps:
Salt and vinegar, salt and vinegar,
Curry flavour, curry flavour,
Ready salted, ready salted,
Smoky bacon, smoky bacon,
Cheese and onion, cheese and onion.
Christine Crump has crunched them.

Christine Crump is feeling sick . . .
Poor old Christine, poor old Christine,
She has indigestion.

Colin West

Through the Teeth

Through the teeth
And past the gums
Look out stomach,
Here it comes!

Anon

Maa-a-a

Maa-a-a?
Yes, my dear.
Maaaaa-a-a?
Yes, my dear.
Maa-aa, do plums have legs?
No, my dear.
Then danged if I ain't ate a snoddywig!

Anon

Chips

They don't have any stones
They don't have any pips
They don't have any bones
That's why I like chips.

Julie Holder

Puddin' Song

Oh, who would be a puddin',
   A puddin' in a pot,
A puddin' which is stood on
   A fire which is hot?
Oh sad indeed the lot
Of puddin's in a pot.

I wouldn't be a puddin'
   If I could be a bird,
If I could be a wooden
   Doll, I would'n' say a word.
Yes, I have often heard
It's grand to be a bird.

But as I am a puddin',
   A puddin' in a pot,
I hope you get the stomachache
   For eatin' me a lot.
I hope you get it hot,
You puddin'-eatin' lot!

Norman Lindsay

My Brother's on the Floor

My brother's on the floor roaring
my brother's on the floor roaring
why is my brother on the floor roaring?
My brother is on the floor roaring
because he's supposed to finish his beans
before he has his pudding.

But he doesn't want to finish his beans
before he has his pudding

he says he wants his pudding
NOW.

But they won't let him

so now my brother is . . . on the floor roaring.

They're saying
I give you one more chance to finish those beans
or you don't go to Tony's
but he's not listening because . . .
he's on the floor roaring.

He's getting told off
I'm not
I've eaten my beans.

Do you know what I'm doing now?
I'm eating my pudding
and . . . he's on the floor roaring.

If he wasn't . . . on the floor roaring
he'd see me eating my pudding
and if he looked really close
he might see a little tiny smile
just at the corner of my mouth.
But he's not looking . . .
he's on the floor roaring.

The pudding is OK
it's not wonderful
not wonderful enough
to be sitting on the floor and roaring about
unless you're my brother.

Michael Rosen

Brother

I had a little brother
And I brought him to my mother
And I said I want another
Little brother for a change.
But she said don't be a bother
So I took him to my father
And I said this little bother
Of a brother's very strange.

But he said one little brother
Is exactly like another
And every little brother
Misbehaves a bit he said.
So I took the little bother
From my mother and my father
And I put the little bother
Of a brother back to bed.

Mary Ann Hobermann

Mum is Having a Baby

Mum is having a baby!
I'm shocked! I'm all at sea!
What's she want another one for:
WHAT'S THE MATTER WITH ME?

Colin McNaughton

Willie Built a Guillotine

Willie built a guillotine,
Tried it out on sister Jean.
Said Mother as she got the mop:
"These messy games have got to stop!"

William E. Engel

An Accident Happened to My Brother Jim

An accident happened to my brother Jim
When somebody threw a tomato at him –
Tomatoes are juicy and don't hurt the skin,
But this one was specially packed in a tin.

Anon

23

Adventures of Isabel

Isabel met an enormous bear,
Isabel, Isabel, didn't care;
The bear was hungry, the bear was ravenous,
The bear's big mouth was cruel and cavernous.
The bear said, "Isabel, glad to meet you,
How do, Isabel, now I'll eat you!"
Isabel, Isabel, didn't worry,
Isabel didn't scream or scurry.
She washed her hands and she straightened her hair up
Then Isabel quietly ate the bear up.

Once in a night as black as pitch
Isabel met a wicked old witch.
The witch's face was cross and wrinkled,
The witch's gums with teeth were sprinkled.
"Ho ho, Isabel!" the old witch crowed,
"I'll turn you into an ugly toad!"
Isabel, Isabel, didn't worry,
Isabel didn't scream or scurry,
She showed no rage and she showed no rancour,
But she turned the witch into milk and drank her.

Isabel met a hideous giant,
Isabel continued self-reliant.
The giant was hairy, the giant was horrid,
He had one eye in the middle of his forehead.
"Good morning, Isabel," the giant said,
"I'll grind your bones to make my bread."
Isabel, Isabel, didn't worry,
Isabel didn't scream or scurry.
She nibbled the zwieback that she always fed off,
And when it was gone, she cut the giant's head off.

Isabel met a troublesome doctor,
He punched and he poked till he really shocked her.
The doctor's talk was of coughs and chills
And the doctor's satchel bulged with pills.
The doctor said unto Isabel,
"Swallow this, it will make you well."
Isabel, Isabel, didn't worry,
Isabel didn't scream or scurry.
She took those pills from the pill concoctor,
And Isabel calmly cured the doctor.

Isabel once was asleep in bed
When a horrible dream crawled into her head.
It was worse than a dinosaur, worse than a shark,
Worse than an octopus oozing in the dark.
"Boo!" said the dream, with a dreadful grin,
"I'm going to scare you out of your skin!"
Isabel, Isabel, didn't worry,
Isabel didn't scream or scurry,
Isabel had a cleverer scheme;
She just woke up and fooled that dream.

Whenever you meet a bugaboo
Remember what Isabel used to do.
Don't scream when the bugaboo says "Boo!"
Just look it in the eye and say, "Boo to you!"
That's how to banish a bugaboo;
Isabel did it and so can you!
Boooooo to you.

Ogden Nash

My Cousin Melda

My Cousin Melda
she don't make fun
she ain't afraid of anyone
even mosquitoes
when they bite her
she does bite them back
and say
"Now tell me – HOW YOU LIKE THAT?"

Grace Nichols

Deborah Delora

Deborah Delora, she liked a bit of fun –
She went to the baker's and she bought a penny bun,
Dipped the bun in treacle and threw it at her teacher –
Deborah Delora! What a wicked creature!

Anon

L

I shan't forget that little villain, L,
Who plagued me for a year in Class 4C.
She used to take delight in raising hell.

Her name I won't reveal – it's just as well
To hide the dreadful child's identity.
I shan't forget that little villain, L.

The fire-alarm went off – she rang the bell
After she locked me in the lavatory.
She used to take delight in raising hell.

The day we went pond-dipping, in she fell!
She couldn't swim, though I could, luckily.
I shan't forget that little villain, L.

She let the gerbils out – they ran pell-mell.
Miss Pringle ended up in Casualty.
She used to take delight in raising hell.

Although she was a problem, truth to tell,
I missed her when she ran away to sea.
I shan't forget that little villain, L.
She used to take delight in raising hell.

Sue Cowling

There Was a Naughty Boy

. . . There was a naughty Boy,
  And a naughty Boy was he,
He ran away to Scotland
  The people for to see –
    There he found
    That the ground
    Was as hard,
    That a yard
    Was as long,
    That a song
    Was as merry,
    That a cherry
    Was as red –
    That lead
    Was as weighty,
    That fourscore
    Was as eighty,
    That a door
    Was as wooden
    As in England –
So he stood in his shoes
  And he wondered,
    He wondered,
He stood in his shoes
  And he wondered.

John Keats

Into the Mixer

Into the mixer he went,
   the nosy boy,
into the mess of wet cement,
   round and round
   with a glugging sound
and a boyish screamed complaint.

Out of the mixer he came,
   the concrete boy,
onto the road made of the same
   quick-setting stuff.
   He looked rough
and he'd only himself to blame.

Matthew Sweeney

The Human Siren

Tim, Tim, the human siren,
LOUDEST boy in town.
Tim, Tim, the human siren,
Never lets you down.

Tim, Tim, the human siren,
When he's not at play,
We rent him to the fire brigade
At fifteen pounds a day.

Colin McNaughton

30

I Din Do Nuttin

I din do nuttin
I din do nuttin
I din do nuttin
All I did
was throw Granny pin
in the rubbish bin.

I din do nuttin
I din do nuttin
I din do nuttin
All I did
was mix paint in
Mammy biscuit tin.

I din do nuttin
I din do nuttin.

John Agard

Why Did the Children

"Why did the children
put beans in their ears
when the one thing we told the children
they must not do
was put beans in their ears?"

"Why did the children
pour molasses on the cat
when the one thing we told the children
they must not do
was pour molasses on the cat?"

Carl Sandburg

Endless Chant

"Who put the overalls in Mrs Murphy's chowder?"
Nobody answered, so she said it all the louder:
"Who put the overalls in Mrs Murphy's chowder?"
Nobody answered, so she said it all the louder:
"Who put the overalls in Mrs Murphy's chowder?"
Nobody answered, so she said it all the louder:
"Who put the overalls in Mrs Murphy's chowder?"
Nobody answered, so she said it all the louder:
"Who put the overalls in Mrs Murphy's chowder?"
Nobody answered, so she said it all the louder:
"Who put the overalls in Mrs Murphy's chowder?"
Nobody answered, so she said it all the louder:
"Who put the overalls in Mrs Murphy's chowder?"
Nobody answered, so she said it all the louder:
"Who put the overalls in Mrs Murphy's chowder?"
Nobody answered, so she said it all the louder:
"Who put the overalls in Mrs Murphy's chowder?"
Nobody answered, so she said it all the louder:
"Who put the overalls in Mrs Murphy's chowder?"
Nobody answered, so she said it all the louder:
"Who put the overalls in Mrs Murphy's chowder?"

Nobody answered, so she said it all the louder:
"Who put the overalls in Mrs Murphy's chowder?"
Nobody answered, so she said it all the louder:
"Who put the overalls in Mrs Murphy's chowder?"
Nobody answered, so she said it all the louder:
"Who put the overalls in Mrs Murphy's chowder?"
Nobody answered, so she said it all the louder:
"Who put the overalls in Mrs Murphy's chowder?"
Nobody answered, so she said it all the louder:
"Who put the overalls in Mrs Murphy's chowder?"
Nobody answered, so she said it all the louder:
"Who put the overalls in Mrs Murphy's chowder?"
Nobody answered, so she said it all the louder:
"Who put the overalls in Mrs Murphy's chowder?"
Nobody answered, so she said it all the louder:
"Who put the overalls in Mrs Murphy's chowder?"
Nobody answered, so she said it all the louder:
"Who put the overalls in Mrs Murphy's chowder?"
Nobody answered, so she said it all the louder:
"Who put the overalls in Mrs Murphy's chowder?"

Anon

Monday's Child is Red and Spotty

Monday's child is red and spotty,
Tuesday's child won't use the potty.
Wednesday's child won't go to bed,
Thursday's child will not be fed.
Friday's child breaks all his toys,
Saturday's child makes an awful noise.
And the child that's born on the seventh day
Is a pain in the neck like the rest, OK!

Colin McNaughton

34

I'm in a Rotten Mood

I'm in a rotten mood today,
a really rotten mood today,
I'm feeling cross,
I'm feeling mean,
I'm jumpy as a jumping bean,
I have an awful attitude –
I'M IN A ROTTEN MOOD!

I'm in a rotten mood today,
a really rotten mood today,
I'm in a snit,
I'm in a stew,
there's nothing that I care to do
but sit all by myself and brood –
I'M IN A ROTTEN MOOD!

I'm in a rotten mood today,
a really rotten mood today,
you'd better stay away from me,
I'm just a lump of misery,
I'm feeling absolutely rude –
I'M IN A ROTTEN MOOD!

Jack Prelutsky

The Song of a Mole

All I did this afternoon was
Dig, dig, dig,
And all I'll do tomorrow will be
Dig, dig, dig,
And yesterday from dusk till dawn
I dug, dug, dug.
I sometimes think I'd rather be
A slug, slug, slug.

Richard Edwards

Sometime the Cow Kick your Head

Sometime the cow kick your head
Sometime she just moo

Even the cow don't know
What she going to do

Until she look at you
Knocked out upon the ground

And she say, "Woo
My leg do that to him"

Andrew J. Grossman

Not a Word

They walked the lane together,
The sky was dotted with stars.
They reached the rails together,
He lifted up the bars.
She neither smiled nor thanked him,
Because she knew not how,
For he was only the farmer's boy
And she was the Jersey cow!

Anon

Commissariat Camels

We haven't a camelty tune of our own
To help us trollop along,
But every neck is a hair-trombone
(*Rtt-ta-ta-ta!* is a hair-trombone!)
And this is our marching-song:
Can't! Don't! Shan't! Won't!
Pass it along the line!
Somebody's pack has slid from his back,
'Wish it were only mine!
Somebody's load has tipped off in the road –
Cheer for a halt and a row!
Urr! Yarrh! Grr! Arrh!
Somebody's catching it now!

Rudyard Kipling

Giraffes Don't Huff

Giraffes don't huff or hoot or howl
They never grump, they never growl
They never roar, they never riot,
They eat green leaves
And just keep quiet.

Karla Kuskin

The Tree Frog

The tree frog
Creaks and croaks and croaks
And says, "Dee deep"
On elms and oaks,
"Dee deep," he says
And stops, till when
It's time to say
"Dee deep" again.

John Travers Moore

What a Wonderful Bird the Frog Are

What a wonderful bird the frog are:–
When he sit, he stand almost;
When he hop, he fly almost.
He ain't got no sense hardly;
He ain't got no tail either,
When he sit, he sit on what he ain't got – almost.

Anon

The Dobermann Dog, O the Dobermann Dog

The Dobermann dog, O the Dobermann dog,
O why did they buy me the Dobermann dog?
he is bigger than I am
by more than a half
and so clumsy at play
it would make a cat laugh –
he sprawls and he falls
over tables and chairs
and goes over his nose when he
stalks down the stairs.
He's the colour of seedcake
mixed with old tar
and he never knows rightly
where his feet are –
he growls in a fashion
to bully all Britain
but it doesn't so much as
frighten my kitten.
On the table at tea-time
he rests his big jaw
and rolls his gentle eyes
for one crumb more.

How often he tumbles me
on the green lawn
then he licks me and stands
looking rather forlorn
like a cockadoo waiting the
sun in the morn.
I call him my Dobe
O my Dobermann dog
my Obermann Dobermann
yes, my Octobermann
Obermann Dobermann Dog.

George Barker

Literalist

R U A B I C?
O O U R A B!

John Fandel

41

Question

Do you love me
Or do you not?
You told me once
But I forgot.

Anon

It's Hard to Lose Your Lover

It's hard to lose your lover
When your heart is full of hope
But it's worse to lose your towel
When your eyes are full of soap.

Anon

When you Get Married

When you get married,
And your husband gets cross,
Just pick up the broom
And ask who's boss.

Anon

Friendship

I've discovered a way to stay friends for ever –
There's really nothing to it.
I simply tell you what to do
And you do it!

Shel Silverstein

The Leader

I wanna be the leader
I wanna be the leader
Can I be the leader?
Can I? Can I?
Promise? Promise?
Yippee, I'm the leader
I'm the leader

OK what shall we do?

Roger McGough

Mr Skinner

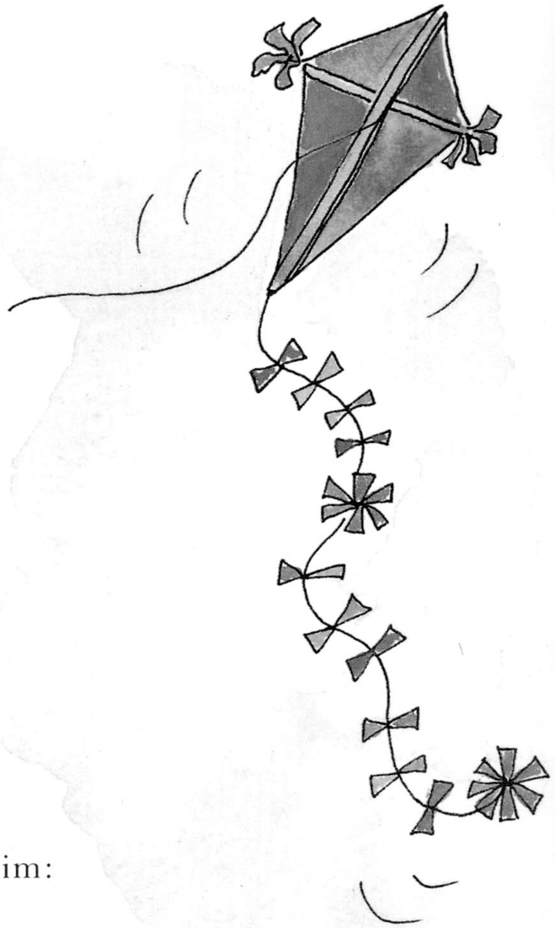

Orville Skinner
(kite-string spinner)
never stopped
to eat his dinner,
for he found it
too exciting
and rewarding
to go kiting.

Flying kites,
he used to sing:
"I'm a spinner
on a string!"
When they warned him:
"Mister Skinner,
capable
but high-strung spinner,
it may take you
to Brazil,"
Skinner cried:
"I hope it will!"

N. M. Bodecker

There Was an Old Woman

There was an old woman of Chester-le-Street
Who chased a policeman all over his beat.

She shattered his helmet and tattered his clothes
And knocked his new spectacles clean off his nose.

"I'm afraid," said the Judge, "I must make it quite clear
You can't get away with that sort of thing here."

"I can and I will," the old woman she said,
"And I don't give a fig for your water and bread.

"I don't give a hoot for your cold prison cell,
And your bolts and your bars and your handcuffs as well.

"I've never been one to do just as I'm bid.
You can put me in jail for a year!"
                                    So they did.

Charles Causley

The Burglar

When the burglar went out
to burgle a house

When the burglar pulled on
his black polo-neck,
his beret, his Reeboks

When the burglar rattled
his skeleton keys,
checked he had his street-map,
said goodbye to his budgie

When the burglar shouldered
an empty bag, big enough
to take as much swag
as the burglar could carry

When the burglar waited
for the bus

When the burglar stood
at the bottom of the street
where the house he'd picked
to burgle was

When the burglar burgled
he didn't know
that another burglar
was inside *his* house

And only the budgie would see

Matthew Sweeney

The Village Burglar

Under the spreading gooseberry bush
  The village burglar lies;
The burglar is a hairy man
  With whiskers round his eyes.

He goes to church on Sundays;
  He hears the Parson shout;
He puts a penny in the plate
  And takes a shilling out.

Anon

Bad Sir Brian Botany

Sir Brian had a battleaxe with great big knobs on;
   He went among the villagers and blipped them on
      the head.
On Wednesday and on Saturday, but mostly on the
      latter day,
   He called at all the cottages, and this is what he said:
      "I am Sir Brian!" (*ting-ling*)
       "I am Sir Brian!" (*rat-tat*)
      "I am Sir Brian, as bold as a lion –
        Take *that!* – and *that!* – and *that!*"

Sir Brian had a pair of boots with great big spurs on,
   A fighting pair of which he was particularly fond.
On Tuesday and on Friday, just to make the street look
      tidy,
   He'd collect the passing villagers and kick them in
      the pond.
      "I am Sir Brian!" (*sper-lash!*)
       "I am Sir Brian!" (*sper-lash!*)
      "I am Sir Brian, as bold as a lion –
        Is anyone else for a wash?"

Sir Brian woke one morning, and he couldn't find his
      battleaxe;
   He walked into the village in his second pair of
      boots.
He had gone a hundred paces, when the street was full
      of faces,
   And the villagers were round him with ironical
      salutes.

"You are Sir Brian? Indeed!
    You are Sir Brian? Dear, dear!
You are Sir Brian, as bold as a lion?
    Delighted to meet you here!"

Sir Brian went a journey, and he found a lot of duck-
        weed:
    They pulled him out and dried him, and they blipped
        him on the head.
They took him by the breeches, and they hurled him
        into ditches,
    And they pushed him under waterfalls, and this is
        what they said:
        "You are Sir Brian – don't laugh,
            You are Sir Brian – don't cry;
        You are Sir Brian, as bold as a lion –
            Sir Brian, the lion, good-bye!"

Sir Brian struggled home again, and chopped up his
    battleaxe,
    Sir Brian took his fighting boots, and threw them in
      the fire.
He is quite a different person now he hasn't got his
    spurs on,
    And he goes about the village as B. Botany, Esquire.

    "I am Sir Brian? Oh, *no!*
        I am Sir Brian? Who's he?
    I haven't got any title, I'm Botany –
        Plain Mr Botany (B)."

A. A. Milne

A Tragic Story

There liv'd a sage in days of yore
And he a handsome pigtail wore,
And wonder'd much and sorrow'd more,
Because it hung behind him.

He mus'd upon this curious case,
And swore he'd change the pigtail's place,
And have it hanging at his face,
Not dangling there behind him.

Says he, "The mystery I've found –
I'll turn me round."
He turned him round,
But still it hung behind him.

Then round and round, and out and in,
All day the puzzled sage did spin;
In vain – it matter'd not a pin,
The pigtail hung behind him.

And right and left, and round about,
And up and down, and in and out
He turn'd, but still the pigtail stout
Hung steadily behind him.

And though his efforts never slack,
And though he twist, and twirl, and tack,
Alas! still faithful to his back,
The pigtail hangs behind him.

William Makepeace Thackeray

A Tone-Deaf Old Person of Tring

A tone-deaf old person of Tring,
When somebody asked him to sing,
    Replied: "It is odd,
    But I cannot tell *God*
Save the Weasel from *Pop Goes the King*."

Anon

Song Sung by a Man on a Barge to another Man on a Different Barge in Order to Drive Him Mad

Oh,

I am the best bargee bar none,
You are the best bargee bar one!
You are the second-best bargee,
You are the best bargee bar me!

Oh,

I am the best . . .

(and so on, until he is
hurled into the canal)

Kit Wright

Tongue Twister

A canner exceedingly canny
One morning remarked to his granny
    "A canner can can
    Anything that he can,
But a canner can't can a can, can he?"

Carolyn Wells

Mr Lott's Allotment

Mr Lott's allotment
Meant a lot to Mr Lott.
Now Mr Lott is missed a lot
On Mr Lott's allotment.

Colin West

The Wizard Said:

"You find a sheltered spot that faces south. . ."
  "And then?"
"You sniff and put two fingers in your mouth . . . "
  "And then?"
"You close your eyes and roll your eye-balls round . . . "
  "And then?"
"You lift your left foot slowly off the ground . . . "
  "And then?"
"You make your palm into a kind of cup . . . "
  "And then?"
"You *very quickly* raise your right foot up . . . "
  "And then?"
"You fall over."

Its Fangs Were Red

Its fangs were red with bloody gore,
its eyes were red with menace,
it battered down my bedroom door,
and burst across my bedroom floor,
and with a loud, resounding roar
said, "ANYONE FOR TENNIS?"

Jack Prelutsky

Hurk

I'd rather play tennis than go to the dentist.
I'd rather play soccer than go to the doctor.
I'd rather play Hurk than go to work.
Hurk? Hurk? What's Hurk?
I don't know, but it *must* be better than work.

Shel Silverstein

Schoolitis

You haven't got a cough,
You haven't got mumps,
You haven't got a chill
Or any funny lumps.
You haven't got a tummy-ache,
You haven't got a fever,
You haven't got a runny nose
Or chicken-pox either.
You don't look a ruin,
You don't look a wreck,
You haven't got toothache
Or a pain in the neck.
You're fit as a fiddle,
You're sound as a bell,
In fact I've never ever
Seen you looking so well!
You don't fool me,
I'm no fool.
Now up out of bed
AND OFF TO SCHOOL!

Brian Patten

54

Late

You're late, said miss.
The bell has gone,
dinner numbers done
and work begun.

What have you got to say for yourself?

Well, it's like this, miss.
Me mum was sick,
me dad fell down the stairs,
the wheel fell off me bike
and then we lost our Billy's snake
behind the kitchen chairs. Earache
struck down me grampy, me gran
took quite a funny turn.
Then on the way I met this man
whose dog attacked me shin –
look, miss, you can see the blood,
it doesn't look too good,
does it?

Yes, yes, sit down –
and next time say you're sorry
for disturbing all the class.
Now, get on with your story,
fast!

Please miss, I've got nothing to write about.

Judith Nicholls

Eeyore's Poem

Christopher Robin is going.
At least I think he is.
Where?
Nobody knows.
But he is going –
I mean he goes
(*To rhyme with "knows"*)
Do we care?
(*To rhyme with "where"*)
We do
Very much.
(*I haven't got a rhyme for that
    "is" in the second line yet.*
Bother.)
(Now I haven't got a rhyme for
    bother. Bother.)
Those two bothers will have
    to rhyme with each other
Buther.
The fact is this is more difficult
    than I thought,
I ought –
(*Very good indeed*)
I ought
To begin again,
But it is easier
To stop.

Christopher Robin, good-bye,
I
(*Good*)
I
And all your friends
Sends –
I mean all your friend
Send –

(*Very awkward this, it keeps
    going wrong.*)
Well, anyhow, we send
Our love
END.

"If anybody wants to clap," said Eeyore when
he had read this, "now is the time to do it."

A. A. Milne

An Attempt at Unrhymed Verse

People tell you all the time,
Poems do not have to rhyme.
It's often better if they don't
And I'm determined this one won't.
                              Oh dear.
Never mind, I'll start again,
Busy, busy with my pen . . . cil.
I can do it, if I try —
Easy, peasy, pudding and gherkins.

Writing verse is so much fun,
Cheering as the summer weather,
Makes you feel alert and bright,
'Specially when you get it more or less the way you want it.

Wendy Cope

28th January

New Leaf

Today is the first day of my new book.
I've written the date
and underlined it
in red felt-tip
with a ruler.
I'm going to be different
with this book.
With this book
I'm going to be good.
With this book

I'm always going to do the date like that
dead neat
with a ruler
just like Christine Robinson.

With this book
I'll be as clever as Graham Holden,
get all my sums right, be as
neat as Mark Veitch;
I'll keep my pens and pencils
in a pencil case
and never have to borrow again.

C.R.

M.V.

OUR dog

Graham Holden
is a swot

58

Miss

With this book
I'm going to work hard,
not talk, be different –
with this book,
not yell out, mess about,
be silly –
with this book.

With this book
I'll be grown-up, sensible,
and every one will want me;
I'll be picked out first
like Iain Cartwright:
no one will ever laugh at me again.
Everything will be
different

with this book . . .

Mick Gowar

← P.E.
teacher

What Is This Here?

With my hands on my head, what is this here?
This is my THINKER, right over here.
That's what I learned in school.

With my hands on my head, what is this here?
This is my I-SEE-YOU, right over here.
Thinker, I-see-you, hinky dinky do.
That's what I learned in school.

With my hands on my head, what is this here?
This is my SNEEZE-MAKER, right over here.
Thinker, I-see-you, sneeze-maker, hinky dinky do.
That's what I learned in school.

With my hands on my head, what is this here?
This is my SOUP STRAINER, right over here.
Thinker, I-see-you, sneeze-maker, soup strainer,
   hinky dinky do.
That's what I learned in school.

With my hands on my neck, what is this here?
This is my COLLAR HOLDER, right over here.
Thinker, I-see-you, sneeze-maker, soup strainer,
   collar holder, hinky dinky do.
That's what I learned in school.

With my hands on my body, what is this here?
This is my BREAD BASKET, right over here.
Thinker, I-see-you, sneeze-maker, soup strainer,
    collar holder, bread basket, hinky dinky do.
That's what I learned in school.

With my hands on my body, what is this here?
This is my BELT HOLDER, right over here.
Thinker, I-see-you, sneeze-maker, soup strainer,
    collar holder, bread basket, belt holder,
    hinky dinky do.
That's what I learned in school.

With my hands on my legs, what is this here?
This is my KNEE CAPPER, right over here.
Thinker, I-see-you, sneeze-maker, soup strainer,
    collar holder, bread basket, belt holder, knee
    capper, hinky dinky do.
That's what I learned in school.

With my hands on my feet, what is this here?
This is my SHOE HOLDER, right over here.
Thinker, I-see-you, sneeze-maker, soup strainer,
    collar holder, bread basket, belt holder, knee
    capper, shoe holder, hinky dinky do.
That's what I learned in school.

Anon

The Head's Hideout

The Head crouched in his hideout
Beneath a dustbin lid.
"I want to see," he muttered,
"No teacher and no kid,

"No parent, no inspector,
Never a district nurse,
And, please, not one school dinner:
The things are getting worse!"

All morning, as the phone rang,
He hid away. Instead:
"The Head is in the dustbin,"
The secretary said.

I'm afraid the Head is in the dustbin..

In the DUSTBIN?!

BOARD OF GOVERNORS

Yes, in the dustbin. You'll have to call back later...

"The *Head* is in the *dustbin*?"
"Yes, he'll be there all day.
He likes sometimes to manage
A little getaway.

"Last year he went to Holland.
Next year he's off to France.
Today he's in the dustbin.
You have to take your chance."

The Head sprang from the garbage
As end-of-school came round.
He cried, "That's quite the nastiest
Hideaway I've found!

"I think I'll stick to teachers
And kids and parents too.
It's just sometimes I've had enough."
Don't blame him. Do you?

Kit Wright

What the Headteacher Said When He Saw Me Running Out of School at 1.15 p.m. on 21 July Last Year to Buy an Ice Cream from Pellozzi's Van

HEY!*

*This poem is an attempt on three world records at once: the longest title, the longest footnote, and the shortest text of any poem in the western world. It has been lodged with *The Guinness Book of Records.*

Fred Sedgwick

Banananananananana

I thought I'd win the spelling bee
   And get right to the top,
But I started to spell "banana",
   And I didn't know when to stop.

William Cole

Hey Diddle, Diddle

Hey diddle, diddle,
The cat and the fiddle,
The cow jumped over the moon;
The little dog laughed
To see such fun,
And the dish ran away with the chocolate biscuits.

Michael Rosen

Little Miss Muffet Sat on a Tuffet

Little Miss Muffet sat on a tuffet,
Eating her curds and whey.
Along came a spider who sat down beside her
And said, "Whatcha got in the bowl, sweetheart?"

Anon

Twinkle, Twinkle Little Bat

Twinkle, twinkle, little bat!
How I wonder what you're at!
Up above the world you fly,
Like a tea-tray in the sky.
        Twinkle, twinkle . . .

Lewis Carroll

Good King Wenceslas

Good King Wenceslas walked out
    In his mother's garden.
He bumped into a Brussels sprout
    And said "I beg your pardon."

Anon

65

Thirty Days Hath September

Thirty days hath September,
And the rest I can't remember.

Michael Rosen

It's Winter, It's Winter

It's winter, it's winter, it's wonderful winter,
When everyone lounges around in the sun!

It's winter, it's winter, it's wonderful winter,
When everyone's brown like a steak overdone!

It's winter, it's winter, it's wonderful winter,
It's swimming and surfing and hunting for conkers!

It's winter, it's winter, it's wonderful winter,
And I am completely and utterly bonkers!

66   *Kit Wright*

Frost on the Flower

Frost on the flower,
Leaf and frond,
Snow on the field-path,
Ice on the pond.

Out of the east
A white wind comes.
Hail on the rooftop
Kettledrums.

Snow-fog wanders
Hollow and hill.
Along the valley
The stream is still.

Thunder and lightning.
Down slaps the rain.
No doubt about it.
Summer again.

Charles Causley

August

The sprinkler twirls.
    The summer wanes.
The pavement wears
    Popsicle stains.

The playground grass
    Is worn to dust.
The weary swings
    Creak, creak with rust.

The trees are bored
    With being green.
Some people leave
    The local scene

And go to seaside
    Bungalows
And take off nearly
    All their clothes.

John Updike

Whether the Weather

Whether the weather be fine
Or whether the weather be not
Whether the weather be cold
Or whether the weather be hot –
We'll weather the weather
Whatever the weather
Whether we like it or not!

Anon

The Sunlight Falls Upon the Grass

The sunlight falls upon the grass;
It falls upon the tower;
Upon my spectacles of brass
It falls with all its power.

It falls on everything it can,
For that is how it's made;
And it would fall on me, except,
That I am in the shade.

Mervyn Peake

'Twas in the Month of Liverpool

'Twas in the month of Liverpool
In the city of July,
The snow was raining heavily,
The streets were very dry.
The flowers were sweetly singing,
The birds were in full bloom,
As I went down the cellar
To sweep an upstairs room.

Anon

The Rain

The rain it raineth on the just
And also on the unjust fella.
But chiefly on the just, because
The unjust steals the just's umbrella.

Baron Charles Bowen

The Storm Starts

The storm starts
when the drops start dropping.
When the drops stop dropping
then the storm starts stopping.

Dr Seuss

Mud

I like mud.
    I like it on my clothes.
I like it on my fingers.
    I like it on my toes.

Dirt's pretty ordinary
    And dust's a dud.
For a really good mess-up
    I like mud.

John Smith

The Mississippi

I am Old Man Mississippi,
full of Time and Mud –
you all must be pretty nippy
if I ever flood!
Swim in me? You would be dippy!
Foolish flesh and blood
would end woeful, dead and drippy!
Keep your distance, bud!

Gavin Ewart

Went to the River

Went to the river, couldn't get across,
Paid five dollars for an old gray hoss.
Hoss wouldn't pull so I traded for a bull.
Bull wouldn't holler so I traded for a dollar.
Dollar wouldn't pass so I threw it on the grass.
Grass wouldn't grow so I traded for a hoe.
Hoe wouldn't dig so I traded for a pig.
Pig wouldn't squeal so I traded for a wheel.
Wheel wouldn't run so I traded for a gun.
Gun wouldn't shoot so I traded for a boot.
Boot wouldn't fit so I thought I'd better quit.
So I quit.

Anon

Daddy Fell into the Pond

Everyone grumbled. The sky was grey.
We had nothing to do and nothing to say.
We were nearing the end of a dismal day.
And there seemed to be nothing beyond,
   Then
      Daddy fell into the pond!

And everyone's face grew merry and bright,
And Timothy danced for sheer delight.
"Give me the camera, quick, oh quick!
He's crawling out of the duckweed!" Click!

Then the gardener suddenly slapped his knee,
And doubled up, shaking silently,
And the ducks all quacked as if they were daft,
And it sounded as if the old drake laughed.
Oh, there wasn't a thing that didn't respond
   When
      Daddy fell into the pond!

Alfred Noyes

The Train to Glasgow

Here is the train to Glasgow.

Here is the driver,
Mr MacIver,
Who drove the train to Glasgow.

Here is the guard from Donibristle
Who waved his flag and blew his whistle
To tell the driver,
Mr MacIver,
To start the train to Glasgow.

Here is a boy called Donald MacBrain
Who came to the station to catch the train
But saw the guard from Donibristle
Wave his flag and blow his whistle
To tell the driver,
Mr MacIver,
To start the train to Glasgow.

Here is the guard, a kindly man
Who, at the last moment, hauled into the van
That fortunate boy called Donald MacBrain
Who came to the station to catch the train
But saw the guard from Donibristle
Wave his flag and blow his whistle
To tell the driver,
Mr MacIver,
To start the train to Glasgow.

73

Here are hens and here are cocks,
Clucking and crowing inside a box,
In charge of the guard, that kindly man
Who, at the last moment, hauled into the van
That fortunate boy called Donald MacBrain
Who came to the station to catch the train
But saw the guard from Donibristle
Wave his flag and blow his whistle
To tell the driver,
Mr MacIver,
To start the train to Glasgow.

Here is the train. It gave a jolt
Which loosened a catch and loosened a bolt,
And let out the hens and let out the cocks,
Clucking and crowing out of their box,
In charge of the guard, that kindly man
Who, at the last moment, hauled into the van
That fortunate boy called Donald MacBrain
Who came to the station to catch the train
But saw the guard from Donibristle
Wave his flag and blow his whistle.
To tell the driver,
Mr MacIver,
To start the train to Glasgow.

The guard chased a hen and, missing it, fell.
The hens were all squawking, the cocks were as well,
And unless you were there you haven't a notion
The flurry, the fuss, the noise and commotion
Caused by the train which gave a jolt
And loosened a catch and loosened a bolt
And let out the hens and let out the cocks,
Clucking and crowing out of their box,
In charge of the guard, that kindly man
Who, at the last moment, hauled into the van
That fortunate boy called Donald MacBrain
Who came to the station to catch the train
But saw the guard from Donibristle
Wave his flag and blow his whistle
To tell the driver,
Mr MacIver,
To start the train to Glasgow.

Now Donald was quick and Donald was neat
And Donald was nimble on his feet.
He caught the hens and he caught the cocks
And he put them back in their great big box.
The guard was pleased as pleased could be
And invited Donald to come to tea
On Saturday, at Donibristle,
And let him blow his lovely whistle,
And said in all his life he'd never
Seen a boy so quick and clever,
And so did the driver,
Mr MacIver,
Who drove the train to Glasgow.

Wilma Horsbrugh

Let Basil Go to Basildon

Let Basil go to Basildon,
Let Lester go to Leicester;
Let Steven go to Stevenage
With raincoat and sou'wester.

Let Peter go to Peterhead,
Let Dudley go to Dudley;
Let Milton go to Milton Keynes –
The pavements there are puddly.

Let Felix go to Felixstowe,
Let Barry go to Barry;
Let Mabel go to Mablethorpe,
But I at home shall tarry.

Let Alice go to Alice Springs,
Let Florence go to Florence;
Let Benny go to Benidorm
Where rain comes down in torrents.

Let Winnie go to Winnipeg,
Let Sidney go to Sydney;
Let Otto go to Ottawa –
I am not of that kidney.

Let Vera go to Veracruz,
Let Nancy go to Nancy,
But I'll stay home while others roam –
Abroad I do not fancy.

Colin West

76

> Morning, Mrs McCave, letter for Dave...

Too Many Daves

Did I ever tell you that Mrs McCave
Had twenty-three sons and she named them all Dave?
Well, she did. And that wasn't a smart thing to do.
You see, when she wants one and calls out, "Yoo-Hoo!
Come into the house, Dave!" she doesn't get *one*.
All twenty-three Daves of hers come on the run!
This makes things quite difficult at the McCaves'
As you can imagine, with so many Daves.
And often she wishes that, when they were born,
She had named one of them Bodkin Van Horn
And one of them Hoos-Foos. And one of them Snimm.
And one of them Hot-Shot. And one Sunny Jim.
And one of them Shadrack. And one of them Blinkey.
And one of them Stuffy. And one of them Stinkey.
Another one Putt-Putt. Another one Moon Face.
Another one Marvin O'Gravel Balloon Face.
And one of them Ziggy. And one Soggy Muff.
One Buffalo Bill. And one Biffalo Buff.
And one of them Sneepy. And one Weepy Weed.
And one Paris Garters. And one Harris Tweed.
And one of them Sir Michael Carmichael Zutt
And one of them Oliver Boliver Butt
And one of them Zanzibar Buck-Buck McFate . . .
But she didn't do it. And now it's too late.

Dr Seuss

Acknowledgements

'I Din Do Nuttin' by John Agard from I DIN DO NUTTIN, published by Hutchinson and reprinted by permission of The Random Century Group; 'The Dobermann Dog' by George Barker from RUNES AND RHYMES AND TUNES AND CHIMES, published by and reprinted by permission of Faber and Faber Limited; 'Mr Skinner' by N M Bodecker from LET'S MARRY SAID THE CHERRY, published by and reprinted by permission of Faber and Faber Limited; 'Frost on the Flower' by Charles Causley from THE YOUNG MAN OF CURY, published by Macmillan and reprinted by permission of David Higham Associates; 'There Was an Old Woman' by Charles Causley from EARLY IN THE MORNING, published by Macmillan and reprinted by permission of David Higham Associates; 'Banananananananana' © 1977 William Cole; 'An Attempt at Unrhymed Verse' © Wendy Cope, reprinted by permission of the author; 'Telling' by Wendy Cope from TWIDDLING YOUR THUMBS, published by and reprinted by permission of Faber and Faber Limited; 'L' by Sue Cowling from WHAT IS A KUMQUAT?, published by and reprinted by permission of Faber and Faber Limited; 'The Song of a Mole' by Richard Edwards from THE WORD PARTY, published by Lutterworth Press 1986; 'The Wizard Said' by Richard Edwards from WHISPERS FROM A WARDROBE, published by Lutterworth Press 1987; 'The Mississippi' by Gavin Ewart from THE COLLECTED EWART 1980 – 1990, published by Hutchinson; 'Literalist' © John Fandel; 'New Leaf' by Mick Gowar from THIRD TIME LUCKY © Mick Gowar 1988, published by Viking Kestrel, 1988; 'Sometime the Cow Kick Your Head' © Andrew J. Grossman; 'Brother' by Mary Ann Hobermann from HELLO AND GOODBY, (1959), published by Little Brown and Co and reprinted by permission of Gina Maccoby Literary Agency; 'Chips' © Julie Holder from A VERY FIRST POETRY BOOK, published by Oxford University Press; 'The Train to Glasgow' by Wilma Horsbrugh from CLINKERDUMP, published by Methuen Children's Books and reprinted by permission of Reed Book Services; 'Giraffes Don't Huff' by Karla Kuskin from ROAR AND MORE, published by Harper and Row and reprinted by permission of HarperCollins; 'Puddin' Song' by Norman Lindsay from THE MAGIC PUDDING © Jane Glad 1918, and reprinted by permission of Angus and Robertson Publishers; 'Easy Money' and 'The Leader' by Roger McGough from A PIE IN THE SKY published by Puffin Books, and reprinted by permission of the Peters, Fraser and Dunlop Group; 'Three Riddled Riddles' © Ian McMillan and Martyn Wiley; 'Monday's Child is Red and Spotty' and 'The Human Siren' by Colin McNaughton from THERE'S AN AWFUL LOT OF WEIRDOS IN OUR NEIGHBOURHOOD © 1987 Colin McNaughton, published in the UK by Walker Books Limited; 'Mum is Having a Baby' by Colin McNaughton from WHO'S BEEN SLEEPING IN MY PORRIDGE? © Colin McNaughton, published in the UK by Walker Books Limited; 'Bad Sir Brian Botany' by A.A. Milne from WHEN WE WERE VERY YOUNG, published by Methuen Children's Books and reprinted by permission of Reed Book Services; 'Cottleston Pie' by A.A. Milne from WINNIE THE POOH, published by Methuen Children's Books and reprinted by permission of Reed Book Services; 'Eeyore's Poem' by A.A. Milne from THE HOUSE AT POOH CORNER, published by Methuen Children's Books and reprinted by permission of Reed Book Services; 'The Tree Frog' by John Travers Moore from CINNAMON SEED, copyright © 1967 John Travers Moore, and published by Houghton Mifflin Co.; 'Adventures of Isabel' by Ogden Nash from ADVENTURES OF ISABEL, published by and reprinted by permission of Little Brown and Company; 'My Cousin Melda' © Grace Nichols; 'Late' by Judith Nicholls from MAGIC MIRROR, published by and reprinted by permission of Faber and Faber Limited; 'Schoolitis' by Brian Patten from THAWING FROZEN FROGS, published by Viking and reprinted by permission of Rogers, Coleridge and White Ltd; 'The Sunlight Falls Upon the Grass' by Mervyn Peake, from RHYMES WITHOUT REASON, published by Methuen and reprinted by permission of David Higham Associates; 'I'm in a Rotten Mood' and 'Its Fangs Were Red' by Jack Prelutsky from NEW KID ON THE BLOCK, published by William Heinemann and reprinted by permission of Reed Book Services; 'My Brother's on the Floor Roaring' by Michael Rosen from WHO DREW ON THE BABY'S HEAD? published by Andre Deutsch and reprinted by permission of Scholastic Publications Ltd; 'Hey, Diddle, Diddle' and 'Thirty Days Hath September' by Michael Rosen from HAIRY TALES AND NURSERY CRIMES, published by Andre Deutsch and reprinted by permission of Scholastic Publications Ltd; 'Why Did the Children' by Carl Sandburg from THE PEOPLE, YES, published by and reprinted by permission of Harcourt, Brace and Company; excerpt from 'Oh Can You Say' © 1979 by Dr Seuss and A. S. Geisel, published by HarperCollins and reprinted by permission of Elaine Greene Ltd; 'Too Many Daves' by Dr Seuss from THE SNEETCHES AND OTHER STORIES published by HarperCollins and reprinted by permission of Elaine Greene Ltd; 'What the Headteacher Said When He Saw Me. . .' by Fred Sedgwick from HEY! © Mary Glasgow Publications Ltd, London; 'Friendship' and 'Hurk' from A LIGHT IN THE ATTIC by Shel Silverstein. Copyright © 1981 by Evil Eye Music, Inc. By permission of Edite Kroll Literary Agency; 'Mud' by John Smith, published by Harrap and reprinted by permission of Chambers Publishers; 'The Burglar' and 'Into the Mixer' by Matthew Sweeney from THE FLYING SPRING ONION, published by and reprinted by permission of Faber and Faber Limited; 'August' by John Updike from A CHILD'S CALENDAR, published by Random House and reprinted by permission of Scholastic Publications Ltd; 'Here is the Nose That Smelled Something Sweet' by Clyde Watson from CATCH ME AND KISS ME AND SAY IT AGAIN, published by HarperCollins and reprinted by permission of Curtis Brown Associates Ltd; 'Christine Crump' © Colin West from IT'S FUNNY WHEN YOU LOOK AT IT; 'Let Basil go to Basildon' and 'Mr Lott's Allotment' by Colin West from WHAT WOULD YOU DO WITH A WOBBLE-DE-WOO? published by Hutchinson and reprinted by permission of The Random Century Group; 'The Head's Hideout' by Kit Wright from CAT AMONG THE PIGEONS, copyright © Kit Wright, 1984, 1987. Published by Viking Kestrel, 1987; 'If You're No Good at Cooking' by Kit Wright, from RABBITING ON, published by and reprinted by permission of Lions, an imprint of HarperCollins Publishers Ltd; 'It's Winter, It's Winter' by Kit Wright from HOT DOG, copyright © Kit Wright 1981. Published by Viking Kestrel Books, 1981; 'Song Sung by a Man on a Barge to Another Man on a Different Barge in Order to Drive Him Mad' by Kit Wright from HOT DOG, copyright © Kit Wright, 1981. Published by Viking Kestrel Books, 1981.

Index of authors and first lines

ARRANGING
FLOWERS
NATURALLY

ARRANGING FLOWERS NATURALLY

PAMELA WESTLAND

THE
APPLE
PRESS

A QUINTET BOOK

Published by The Apple Press
6 Blundell Street
London, N7 9BH

ISBN 1-85076-247-3

This book was designed and produced by
Quintet Publishing Limited
6 Blundell Street
London N7 9BH

Creative Director: Terry Jeavons
Art Director: Ian Hunt
Designers: Stuart Walden, Wayne Blades
Project Editor: Judith Simons
Editor: Lisa Cussans
Photographer: Nelson Hargreaves
Flower arrangements and styling: Pamela Westland

Typeset in Great Britain by
Central Southern Typesetters, Eastbourne
Manufactured in Hong Kong by
Regent Publishing Services Limited
Printed in Hong Kong by
Leefung-Asco Printers Limited

CONTENTS

INTRODUCTION

Arranging flowers is one of the oldest of home crafts. It has its origins in the ancient cultures of all parts of the world, when people decorated their places of worship with garlands of flowers and leaves, and placed posies of wild flowers in homage to their deities. Gradually, over the centuries, the joy of arranging flowers extended to the home, and people decked their houses with flowers in celebration of seasonal festivals and special family occasions.

From the very beginning, flower arrangements had a natural ease. They were arranged with grace and charm – with love, even – and it is only comparatively recently that guidelines have been laid down and rules drawn up to place restrictions on just how flowers and foliage are arranged.

This book owes nothing to such limitations, and sets out to show how flowers may be arranged in the most natural way, so that they retain all the beauty they had when growing in the garden or in the wild. For, in the context of arranging flowers naturally, it is recognized that wild flowers have an important role to play. Not only do they evoke the joy of the countryside and greatly extend the range of plant materials available to the arranger; they have a quality, it could be described as an innocence, which is not found in raised and hothouse blooms.

A circlet of flowers in fresh, clear colours makes a delightful table or wall decoration, which can be composed of side shoots and snippings from larger arrangements.

If you have ever found conventional flower arranging too stiff and formal, you will find plenty of inspiration and much to delight you as you work your way through this book. There are sections on the appreciation of colour, and how to relate it to your flower arrangements; on how by blending certain colour groups you can achieve visual effects ranging from the restrained and classic approach to the totally unrestrained and modern idiom; on the wide range of textures there are in plant materials, from the soft and downy appearance of, say, ballota to the high-gloss and light-reflecting surface of, for example, tulip and lily petals. Finally, a section describes the various tools that will help you to develop your skill, and how, with the minimum of special equipment, you can achieve just the look you want in designs of all kinds.

The step-by-step projects will also guide you in the use of colour, shape, texture and form. The materials used in the step-by-step arrangements are all listed, but do not feel you have to rigidly employ the same plant material. Once you begin to assess the colour values and the contrasting textures of plant materials, once you start 'thinking flowers', you will be well on the way to developing your own style of arranging flowers naturally.

Arranging flowers is no longer a pleasure to be reserved for celebrations and holidays, or for when you would like to impress the dinner guests. It is an art that has relevance every day, with flowers to enhance every room, practically every corner, of the home. And when there is something to celebrate, be it Christmas or a wedding in the family, flowers and foliage rise to the occasion and set the scene.

Three full, rounded chrysanthemums hold the visual weight at the base of this russet-coloured design and become the focal point.

CHAPTER ONE

EXPLORING THE POSSIBILITIES

Developing your own sense of harmony, shape, and colour in flower arrangements has all the thrill of experimenting with new fashions – and the results can be just as personal. A flower arrangement should be tailor-made to suit its situation in your home. It should not only be the right size and shape for the space it fills; it should suit your own personality, and even your mood, perfectly. Think of a floral display as both an accessory to your furnishings and a reflection of your own individual style, and then start experimenting to find the types that are absolutely right for you.

Flowers in every colour of the rainbow, and including all three primary and secondary colours, come together in an exciting midsummer arrangement.

Perhaps your style is expressed in the country look, in casual flower groupings that look as if they have been gathered from a colourful garden or a flowery meadow and arranged just the way they are. The look may be summed up for you by, for example, a deep brown glazed pot brimming over with all the profusion of a country garden, perhaps with campanula (bellflower) and mallow, everlasting pea and marigolds, a rich palette of bright colours and varied shapes. Or you might prefer the misty look of a glass jug filled with the exceptionally pretty heads of white wild carrot flowers, like so many snowflakes settled on flat umbrellas. Such a delicate cluster looks its most enchanting when set upon a window-sill, where it will filter the light and provide a perfect transition between the room and the world outside.

In quite a different mood, your interpretation of the country look might be to make small posies of herbs and stand one at every place setting around the table, a tumbling profusion of golden thyme, spiky rosemary, and downy-soft sage leaves, with touches of pink chive, purple marjoram, and white feverfew flowers. You would only need to brush one of the arrangements lightly with your hand to release the mingled scents of the herb garden on a summer's evening – an added bonus in any flower arrangement.

The country look is epitomized not so much by which flowers you use – you may choose a medley of different flower types or a single one – but on how you arrange them. A bunch of daffodils standing in an upright vase is country style. So is a handful of forget-me-nots arranged to trail over the sides of a pottery jar. The 'arrangement' is casual, so casual the flowers appear to have settled themselves in the most natural positions; and the containers are simple. Pottery honey jars, enamel milk churns, earthenware flower pots (fitted with a hidden, water-retaining container), jugs, mugs, and baskets all help to capture the country mood.

THE CLASSIC LOOK

By contrast, you may find that flowers arranged in a classic style come closest to the way you have furnished your home and the look you wish to capture. You might express this style with a rose-patterned bowl holding a dome of pink and red roses, pale green viburnum (arrowwood) flowers, and green-and-pink-tinged hydrangeas – a medley of generous flower shapes in only two delicate pastel colours. In a more assertive scheme, you might go for a blue-and-white urn-shaped vase filled with a cascade of deep red and magenta antirrhinums (snapdragons), dahlias, and zinnias, plus blue larkspur and deepest blue alkanet. The Victorians loved such blends of velvet-rich colours, and they have remained classics ever since. Again, in another mood, you might arrange a tall, barrel-shaped vase with a handful of lilies – white arum lilies, orange day lilies, or pink- and peach-coloured alstroemeria (Peruvian lilies). Lilies of all types have a special place in the art of flower arranging, and always look both classic and elegant.

Here, too, the choice of container plays an important part in the overall style of the arrangement. Deep wide bowls, raised bowls, pedestal plates such as cake stands, tall, slender tapering vases, urn-shaped ones, and those with a generous rounded shape can all be used to achieve a classic elegance. And although you can create an arrangement with wild flowers that says 'classic' all the way, some flowers, roses and lilies especially, are considered more classic than others.

The classic arrangement of spray chrysanthemums, feverfew, and petunias in an old lustre jug echoes the style and feeling of the Oriental wallhanging.

13

MODERN AND BOLD

In complete contrast to both the casual ease of
the country look and the soft elegance of the
classic style, the 'bold' look has all the
excitement and vibrance of a modern abstract
painting. It looks most at home in a room
decorated with plain colours, both neutral and
assertive, deep textures, and the clean, clear
lines of modern furniture. You might express the
bold look with a bright red glass vase filled with
scarlet poppies or gerberas or, more vibrant still,
with a handful of deep blue cornflowers.
Alternatively, you could choose to understate the
colour factor and accentuate the form of the
container. For example, a black-and-white-
striped vase holding a single white arum lily or a
trio of white gerberas would strike a bold note in
any room. Plain containers, black, white, or
grey, or in strong primary or secondary colours,
tall narrow vases with abstract patterns, and
chunky glass jars in geometric shapes – all
contribute to this bold approach to arranging.

GETTING INSPIRED

Once you start 'thinking flowers' you will find
inspiration for arrangements in nearly everything
around you. Whether you are walking in the
countryside, wandering around a garden, looking
through fabric samples and paint swatches,
visiting an art gallery, or even choosing a
greetings card – you'll find that any of these
situations has the potential to fire your
imagination and spark off an idea for a flower
arrangement. It is not a question of slavishly
copying a fabric design or an artist's work, or of
trying to recreate nature indoors. Rather, it's a
matter of seeing combinations of colours and
textures, shapes and forms together – perhaps
seeing them in a new light – and picking up ideas
you can translate into floral displays.

The zingy pink dahlias, as
bright as can be, make a bold
colour statement teamed with
yellow and coral zinnias.

14

    You might, for example, be walking through a

Blue and orange, two
colours that bring out the best
in each other, are used to
good effect in this simple
garden room group.

bluebell wood and be struck, not for the first time, by the breathtaking charm of the blue flowers and their backdrop of green foliage. You cannot, unless you have a private source of bluebells, recreate this scene from nature, but you can capture the colour combination in a variety of ways. A jug of blue grape hyacinths arranged with glossy green leaves; a bright blue beaker filled with mixed green foliage; a bunch of blue flowers placed beside a green curtain, on a window-sill where it will be seen against the background of the lawn outside, or displayed in front of a green wall – each of these ideas uses the colour combination in a different and interesting way.

In a garden you might see a lovely, old-fashioned rose twining around an apple tree stump, and be inspired by the perfection of the complementary textures, the soft, smooth petals side by side with the rough, craggy tree bark. Here is a look you can interpret in any number of ways in flower arrangements throughout the year. In spring, you might group a bunch of daffodils with a couple of bare branches or with a few twigs hanging with catkins, or place a collection of flowering primula plants in a rough-textured wooden basket. In summer, you could recreate the scene almost exactly with stems of full, petally roses arranged around a piece of driftwood. In autumn, you might set out pretty, mop-headed hydrangeas and michaelmas daisies in a container hidden behind a piece of curved tree bark. (Some florists sell bark as a versatile natural accessory.) And in winter, what could be more effective than a collection of thick, knobbly branches and, say, lilies or irises arranged so that, as in the rose scene, each texture emphasizes and complements the other?

You might be passing a florist's shop or a flower stall and get a sudden lift from the sight of bunches and bunches of flowers massed together in buckets, the effect of concentrated colour in an artless form. It is a look that is easy to create

in the home, and especially effective when you are using small or fragile flowers. Take primroses and violets, for example. Each tiny flower is almost too delicate to handle, almost too small to appreciate when placed individually in an arrangement. But take bunches of primroses and violets, shaped into posies and ringed around with their leaves, and the pale, subtle colour of the one and the deep, rich vibrant hue of the other are intensified and the effect magnified a hundred-fold.

Sweet peas are another example. A bunch of sweet peas in mixed colours will always be pretty, creating the soft overall effect of a colour-wash painting. But cluster the flowers together, red with red, mauve with mauve, pink with pink, and arrange them in single-colour bunches, then watch how each hue seems intensified and is seen to perfection.

Arranging flowers in bunches not only emphasizes the individual colours, it can change the apparent shape of the flowers, too. Take, for example, dried pearl everlasting, each flower a tiny creamy-white ball. If you arrange each stem singly among other dried flowers you get a speckled and spotty effect, pinpricks of cream among other, more assertive materials. Yet take a leaf from the florist-shop book by arranging the flowers in bunches, and you have, instead, a massed head of tiny flowers giving the effect of, perhaps, a mophead hydrangea or a head of yarrow composed of small florets. Massed together, these small dried flowers, and others such as pink and white rhodanthe, can stand up to the strongest and boldest competition.

Furnishing materials, both fabrics and wallcoverings, can be positively inspirational and supply many a lead for flower arrangements. You may find yourself drawn to a pattern composed of a profusion of flowers, roses and peonies for instance, or one in which foliage plays the key role. You may find colour combinations you had not thought of trying –

17

■ MOODY BLUES

1 The shallow bowl made of woven rushes is first lined with plastic. A block of soaked foam holds the stems of the hydrangea, hellebores and silver-grey leaves.

2 A white lace-cap hydrangea at the back of the design and more hellebores form a softly rounded dome shape and conceal the foam.

3 The cluster of irises on the left are positioned within the domed outline with one, in half bud, extending the height. This cluster is balanced by the three irises positioned diagonally opposite.

YOU WILL NEED

▉ shallow bowl

▉ plastic, for lining

▉ block of foam

▉ hydrangeas

▉ hellebores

▉ silver-grey foliage

▉ irises

▉ purple sage foliage

19

yellow and pink flowers shown together, or red and mauve, perhaps. Once you begin seeing furnishings, themselves inspired by nature, as a springboard for ideas, you will be longing to interpret them in flower arrangements.

Paintings, both in art galleries and on greetings cards, can have an even more direct influence on your taste in floral designs. No one expects you to go home and copy a Dutch Old Master in chrysanthemums, roses, tulips, poppies, and lilies (for many artists were fond of combining flowers from different seasons). But simply by assessing your preferences in art, you can help to establish your preferences in flower-arranging styles.

FLOWER COLOURS

Looking at all the shades of green in a woodland, at the profusion of flower colours in a well-stocked herbaceous border, and at the whole palette of colours an artist used to paint a picture, both sharpens your awareness of the infinite number of tints, tones, and shades of colours there are in nature and helps you to understand how to use them to the most pleasing effect.

The way you blend the colours of the flowers you use, and the colour of the background against which you place them, makes all the difference as to how each separate flower and the design as a whole is seen. It is not the brightness of each individual flower that determines whether it will be seen in all its pretty detail, but the colours of the flowers and leaves around it. Arrange a bunch of orange, red, and mauve tulips together and none of the colours, not even the red, will appear to dominate the others; the effect will be restrained and easy on the eye. Place those same red tulips in a vase with only green flowers and foliage, or against a green wall, and the brilliance of the colour will be seen in all its glory. As a third experiment, mix the red tulips with yellow and blue flowers and the

Arranged in bunches of each colour – crimson, scarlet, pink, and white – the sweet peas make a powerful and pretty impact.

effect is modern, bold, and strident.

Why is this? The easiest way to understand the inter-relationship of colour, and to use colour combinations in the ways you find most pleasing, is to imagine or draw a colour wheel. Draw a rough circle and divide it into six equal segments, like slices of a cake. Place each of the three primary colours, red, blue and yellow, in alternate segments; these are ones that cannot be produced by mixing other colours together. Fill in the spaces with the colours known as secondaries, those made by mixing two primary colours together. Thus, you place mauve between red and blue, green between blue and yellow, and orange between yellow and red.

To make the wheel more representative of all the gradations of colour in nature, you could colour in the tint and shade of each segment. A tint is the basic hue mixed with white, giving a pastel colour, while a shade is the basic hue mixed with black, giving a deeper tone. So, the red section would comprise pale pink, scarlet, and crimson, and so on around the wheel.

This simple exercise gives you the key to using colour creatively, and composing flower arrangements that have just the effect you want. If your taste is for classic designs in which the colours blend harmoniously, combine tints and shades of a single hue – a design composed of only pink and red flowers, for example – or colours that are next to each other on the wheel. A bowl of yellow daffodils, orange lilies, and red tulips would be an example of this kind of perfect harmony; a bunch of red, mauve, and blue anemones is another.

If, on the other hand, you want to emphasize one particular colour, place it against its opposite colour on the wheel. In this way you can make yellow roses look their most vibrant by surrounding them with mauve flowers; while orange lilies will seem brightest if you partner them with blue flowers, or place them in a blue vase or against a blue wall.

Colours that face each other, or oppose each other on the wheel, are said to be complementary. Those next to each other are, appropriately, termed adjacent, and those that alternate with each other – mauve, green, and orange, for example – are termed triadic. Artists know the effects of combining colours as if by instinct, but it is a talent that can be learned. By mixing and matching scraps of coloured paper or paint sample swatches to see the various effects, and by studying floral pictures and fabrics, you will develop your own eye for colour and be well on the way to making the most pleasing flower arrangements.

CLASSIC FLOWER COMBINATIONS

There are some flower combinations that are so attractive, they have become classic partnerships. If you study the properties of each flower type – the colour, shape, and texture – you will find each one has just what it takes to bring out the best in the other.

Buttercups and daisies are a good example of the classic combination. They spatter the countryside in spring and summer, turning meadows and waysides into green canvases awash with brilliant yellow and crisp white. Arranged in a simple container such as a decorative preserve jar or a small basket, the flowers look just as pretty indoors, the buttercups trailing and twisting over the rim. As a partnership, the two have everything going for them. Yellow and white look fresh and bright

Buttercups and daisies, a classic flower partnership, are supplemented by wild marguerites in the pretty pottery basket design.

▌SWEET PEA SYMPHONY

1 The neck of the apricot-coloured vase, a classic bowl shape, is fitted with crumpled wire-mesh netting. The two-tone flecked carnations are arranged in groups of three.

2 More toning carnations extend the width of the design. The partly opened roses and the geranium give weight at the base, and begin to mask the stem-holding wire.

YOU WILL NEED

- ▌ bowl-shaped vase
- ▌ wire-mesh netting

- ▌ carnations
- ▌ roses
- ▌ geranium flower
- ▌ sweet peas
- ▌ variegated lamium leaves

3 Shell pink, coral and white sweet peas with their twisty-twirling stems give the design its gentle fullness. A few stems of silver and green variegated lamium leaves add a natural touch.

together, evoking rays of golden sunlight, and the flower shapes and textures contrast perfectly. Buttercups are like flat little saucers, shiny, sparkling, and reflecting all the available light; while daisies, just the opposite, are composed of a multitude of matt petals, giving a cut or jagged appearance.

It is this contrast between different shapes and textures, shiny flowers and leaves arranged with matt ones, that heightens the interest in any arrangement. You can translate the simple buttercups-and-daisies theme into other flower types to achieve a similar effect. Full, rounded, and golden yellow ranunculus paired with the simple composite shapes of marguerites or white spray chrysanthemums make an enlarged and sophisticated version of the wild flower partnership, and one that is just as successful. For extra effect, arrange the flowers in a blue-and-white jug or classic vase, and the colour will appear brighter than ever.

Daffodils and tulips are another classic combination, the epitome of springtime. Give way to a sudden impulse to buy a bunch of each on the way home, and you have the makings of another perfect partnership: the daffodils or narcissus with their extended trumpet shape and not-so-shiny petals, and the tulips with their initial barrel shape and high-gloss appearance. As for their colour, you could buy two bunches of flowers every single day while they are in season and still not exhaust all the possible permutations.

For a harmonizing group, try pairing orange-centred daffodils with orange tulips, or pink-centred ones with their exact colour match. The contrasting shapes will ensure that there is 'movement' in the group, and the close colour harmony will lend a classic look.

There will be actual movement among the flowers, too. Don't forget that tulips, more than practically any other flower, need room to 'grow'. As the flowers develop the petals unfurl until they are almost flat, when they will take up about three times their original space. The golden rule to remember when arranging tulips is to be generous, leaving plenty of space to spare.

Roses and carnations are a third classic flower combination, and feature in many a summer bouquet or gift spray. You can mix and match the different flower types to achieve the prettiest partnerships: tightly furled rosebuds with full, rounded carnations; fully-opened cabbage roses with tiny spray carnations; single wild roses and garden pinks, dianthus, a close relation and a flower that, like the carnation, has a long vase life. Arranged in a natural way the classic rose and carnation partnership, however you choose to interpret it, will be one of the prettiest expressions of summer.

The main thing to remember is that, when arranging flowers naturally, there are no rules and regulations, no rights and wrongs. However you choose to arrange the flowers, if the design pleases you and enhances the room, then it is right for you.

Tulips, more than any other flower, need room to 'grow' in a design if they are not to look cramped and crowded.

CHAPTER TWO

TOOLS AND TECHNIQUES

To begin with, you need very little special equipment for flower arranging, just the plant material itself, a container, and a pair of stem scissors or secateurs or pruning shears. But as you progress to use a range of different containers, some with particularly narrow or wide apertures and some as flat as a board, you will need some special materials – known as 'mechanics' – to hold the stems firmly in place. Indeed, it is easier to compose even simple flower arrangements if you have some behind-the-scenes equipment to help you.

An unusual use of stem-holding material: the Chinese lanterns are arranged in a cluster of bamboo stems.

Stem-holding foam is one of the most versatile and useful materials. You can buy it from florists in small cylinders, about 6cm/2½in deep with an 8cm/3in diameter, or in blocks slightly larger than household bricks. Other shapes, such as spheres, cones, and pre-formed rings, will be described in later chapters.

There are two types of foam. One, for use with all fresh flowers and foliage, is absorbent and usually green. You soak it in a bowl of water for a few minutes until it is heavy enough to sink to the bottom and then, when it is ready to use, it will float to the surface again. The other type, usually brown or grey with a sparkly surface, is specially for use with dried flowers and preserved leaves. It is tougher than the absorbent foam, which should never be used dry.

You can buy special plastic saucers with an indentation just the right size to hold one of the foam cylinders, and others, called candle-cups, with the addition of a central plug that fits firmly into the top of a bottle or candlestick. Using one of these saucers of foam enables you to use a whole range of items – narrow-necked vases, teapots, bread boards, and trays, to name a few – for natural-looking arrangements. There is space around the foam to enable you to keep it topped up with water and permanently moist.

The blocks of foam are used for larger designs, in shallow bowls, wide baskets, and hidden containers on top of a pedestal. You can cut them to any size and shape you need, but cut them dry, before soaking, so you can easily store the remainder. Once foam has been soaked and allowed to dry out it will not reabsorb moisture. To store it wet you must put it in a sealed plastic bag or plastic box. Stored in this way, absorbent foam can be re-used, though eventually it becomes too full of holes to take a firm grip on the stems.

The other principal stem-holding material is chicken-wire netting, which is used, crumpled into a ball, in wide-necked containers such as urns and jugs. The irregular holes in the netting enable you to angle stems in ways not possible with an open aperture. The netting to buy is one with a 5cm/2in mesh, which is sold in widths from 30cm/12in. One or two pieces are all you need, as they can be used over and over again.

Another use for the netting is to stretch it over foam in a specially wide container when – in the case of a large pedestal arrangement, for instance – you are using thick, woody stems or heavy branches. The wire gives extra support and avoids any danger of the foam crumbling under pressure.

The choice between using stem-holding foam or crumpled wire netting in the neck of a container – a pretty teapot, say – will depend on the style of arrangement you wish to make. Fitting the aperture with netting simply allows you to place the stems at various angles in an upright position. But foam permits much more versatility. If you use a saucer of foam fixed to the neck of the container, or wedge a cut block into the aperture to extend about 5cm/2in above the rim, you can then place stems at any angle you wish: upright, horizontal, even sloping downwards. Therefore, you would always choose foam if you wanted to compose an arrangement with, say, a triangular shape, or in any design with extended width at the sides.

Pinholders, which are flat, heavy weights available in a wide range of sizes and in round, oval, and rectangular shapes, are useful for arrangements in shallow, water-holding containers such as soup plates or casserole dishes. The close-spaced vertical pins hold the stems firmly at a wide range of angles. An example of an attractive design using this device would be a couple of stems of pale pink apple blossom and a bunch of deep pink tulips arranged in a brown baking dish. A trio of large fleshy leaves or a handful of granite chippings or small pebbles could be used to conceal the pinholder from view.

A host of golden daffodils, narcissi, and tulips heralds the onset of spring from an open doorway. The container, fitted with crumpled wire netting, is an ivy-green casserole dish.

1 A water-holding pinholder is fixed to the wooden board with dabs of florists' clay. The apple blossom stems form an 'L' shape, with sprays of cypress softening the angle.

▌ BLOSSOM TIME

2 The deep pink of the two-tone alstroemeria (Peruvian lilies) echoes the stronger colour in the apple blossom petals. The rose at the base will form the focal point of the design.

3 The cluster of roses softens the severe outlines formed by the apple twigs. The fans of cypress foliage around the base complete the task of concealing the stem holder.

—

YOU WILL NEED

- base
- water-holding pinholder
- florists' clay

- apple-blossom stems
- cypress foliage
- alstroemeria (Peruvian lilies)
- roses

A FIRM FOOTING

No matter what kind of holding material you use, and however simple the arrangement, secure fixing is of the utmost importance. Wobbly stem-holding aids are worse than useless, and could cause a lovely arrangement to collapse or gradually disintegrate before your eyes. Time spent in preparing your container is time well spent, and makes composing the arrangement infinitely easier.

A special extra-tacky florists' clay called Oasis Fix is sold in flat strips, and is invaluable for attaching plastic saucers and other water- or foam-holding containers to stands or bases. It must be used dry, on absolutely dry surfaces, but once in place it will not be dislodged by moisture.

Place three or four dabs of the clay around the base of a candle-cup before pressing it into place on top of a wine carafe, or around a small dish before inserting it in a basket. Press a walnut-sized dab of clay underneath a plastic prong, used to hold foam in place in a water-holding container, and attach small dabs around the edge of heavy pinholders to prevent them from toppling.

For extra security, tape blocks of foam in position in containers (and if the containers are to be placed on stands, tape these down as well) with a special adhesive tape known simply as florists' tape. It is sold in a range of widths and colours, such as brown, green, black, and beige. Criss-cross two strips of the tape over the top of the container and take it well down at the sides. Flowers or foliage positioned to slope downwards or tumble and twist over the container rim will be needed to hide it from view. With large arrangements especially, it is only when the container, foam, crumpled wire, and any additional base or stand look as if they have been tied up like a parcel that they are secure and ready for action!

CHOOSING CONTAINERS

Once you get into the swing of arranging flowers for pleasure, one of the most stimulating aspects is choosing a container. And when you get into the habit of using stem-holding materials, absorbent foam especially, you will soon realize that as far as containers go, the sky's the limit. A container does not have to be a vase, nor even a vessel; it does not need to be waterproof, and even an aperture is not mandatory. Let your imagination run riot, and you will find that practically any decorative or utilitarian item around the home can be pressed into pretty and practical service.

Remember, too, that the art of concealment goes hand in hand with that of flower arranging. A large, fleshy leaf or a flat, round flower placed low down in a design can go a long way towards concealing not only the fixing materials, but any chips, cracks, and other imperfections in the container. This means that junk-shop and flea market bargains can be used with style.

China, glass, and pottery offer endless design opportunities. A spare and even damaged piece of a china set, such as a gravy boat, cream jug, or vegetable dish, makes an ideal container for the centre of a dining table. A teapot or coffee pot – missing lid no obstacle – looks pretty tumbling over with everything from buttercups to roses, and jugs and mugs of all kinds are natural containers. Wine glasses and tumblers make lovely flower holders for individual place settings, and look pretty on the dressing table, too. Instead of using foam or crumpled wire, which would show, partly fill the glasses with gravel chippings or small marbles, which will both tame the stems and become part of the design. Or, in a completely different mood, float a single flower in water in each glass.

Raid the kitchen for more possibilities. Pottery and earthenware casserole dishes have the visual weight to look good with designs

A decorative terracotta teapot holds a cluster of geranium, roses and many-coloured Shirley poppies – a pretty design for a summer's day.

35

1 The glass wine carafe is partially filled with coloured water and fitted with a cylinder of soaked foam held in a plastic saucer. A cascade of broom forms an arched curve.

■ GRACEFUL CURVES

2 The tulips and alstroemeria (Peruvian lilies) follow the outline set by the yellow broom. The single gerbera, its stem cut very short, nestles close to the foam and will become the focal point.

3 From the ovoid outline of the tulips through the trumpets of alstroemeria (Peruvian lilies) to the daisy-like face of the gerbera, the contrasting shapes of the flowers give this simple triangular arrangement its appeal.

YOU WILL NEED

▓ glass wine carafe

▓ cylinder of foam

▓ plastic saucer

▓ florists' clay

▓ florists' tape

▓ food colouring

▓ broom

▓ tulips

▓ alstroemeria (Peruvian lilies)

▓ gerbera

▓ ivy

▓ silver foliage

▓ spray carnations

including branches of blossom, leaves, or berries; and flat baking dishes can be used with the plastic prong and foam combination, or with pinholders, for a variety of upright designs. Storage jars are perfect to casually display a handful of poppies, or use a wooden flour bin with an arrangement of dried grasses and grain.

Decorative trays and chopping boards, wooden bread boards, woven place mats, and flat plates can be used with the plastic saucer and foam partnership for fresh and dried flower arrangements of all kinds. Such containers – or, more accurately, bases – look especially effective when the holding material, and therefore the design, is positioned off-centre.

Baskets and wooden boxes need an inner liner if they are to be arranged with fresh flowers (just a well-secured piece of dry foam for use with dry materials). This is an ideal way to recycle damaged or worn-out bowls, dishes, and baking tins, or to use washed-out food cans or glass jars. An old wooden tea box, work box, or pencil box takes on all the glamour of a casket of jewels when arranged with a cascade of flowers and foliage in precious-stone colours.

The use of a saucer of stem-holding foam brings all manner of unlikely items into the container category: not only wine bottles, carafes, and candlesticks, but discarded lamp bases, cosmetic bottles, upturned wine glasses, decorative chocolate boxes, china ornaments, an old box-Brownie camera – the possibilities are endless. All you need do is to attach the saucer firmly to the improvised container in order to lift the stem-holding foam, and ultimately the flower design, high into the air. One note of caution: fill tall, hollow containers with sand or dry beans first to keep them from being top-heavy.

Start thinking laterally, no holds barred, about flower containers, and there is no limit to the items you can adapt. Food opens up a wealth of new possibilities. Look appraisingly at the colour, texture, and shape of a melon, pumpkin,

watermelon, pineapple, orange, lemon, or grapefruit, and imagine them spilling over with spiralling foliage and colourful flowers. No sooner said than done! Simply scoop out the flesh to hollow out the shell – a curved grapefruit knife is the best tool to use – rinse and dry it, and cut a thin slice from the base so it stands level. Vegetable marrows make two-way containers: you can stand them either horizontally, to make a canoe shape, or upright. Fit the container with a water-holding liner. Round plastic boxes, margarine tubs, and yoghurt pots are suitable for the larger shells. Spice jars and egg cups are a perfect fit for oranges and lemons. Then fit the container with a stem-holding material in the usual way if you need it. For the next week or so, you can treat the shell as any other container.

A decorative puff-type loaf of bread, or its single-serving equivalent, a puff roll, makes a more permanent flower holder. Cut a thin slice from the top and scoop out the bread to leave strong, firm walls. (Use the crumbs in stuffings and toppings.) Bake the shell in a low-temperature oven until it feels light and sounds hollow when tapped. Leave it to cool, then fit it as described for a fruit shell. A bread loaf vase looks wonderful arranged with, for example, marmalade-coloured marigolds, purple pansies, and trails of variegated ivy.

Yet another shell-type container, the quickest and easiest to prepare, is an egg. Crack it near the top, tip out the contents, and wash and dry the shell. Use eggs as miniature vases for tiny flowers like primroses, violets, pulmonaria, and winter aconites. Stand them in egg cups, decorative spice jars, or cosmetic bottles.

As natural as can be, a collection of the showiest garden flowers towering above a sparkling white water jug.

A SENSE OF PROPORTION

What with roses in a tea pot, marigolds in a loaf shell, and primroses in eggcups, you can begin to see that there really is no end to the number of partnerships you can create between containers and plant material. But to bring out the very best in both elements, it is necessary to keep a sense of proportion. A small nosegay of buttercups and daisies would fade into obscurity in a weighty casserole dish, while a generous bunch of dahlias would look top heavy, and may well be so, in a plastic milk jug.

Most people have a built-in awareness of proportions that are agreeable; we don't use the word 'right' because there is no hard and fast rule about it, no fixed proportion of flowers to container that must be followed slavishly. So there is no need to get out your slide rule! There are, however, certain guidelines that will help you to make what looks like a perfect marriage every time you arrange flowers. It is generally agreed that, in a stylized arrangement, the total height of flowers and foliage above the rim of the container should usually be at least one-and-a-half times the height or width (whichever is the greater) of the container itself. This means that if you use a jug 20cm/8in tall, or a vegetable dish 20cm/8in wide, the topmost plant material should extend at least 30cm/12in above the rim.

The one-and-a-half to one (or, if it's easier to calculate, three to two) ratio applies equally to horizontal arrangements. Whenever the width of a design is greater than the height – when you compose a long, low arrangement for the dining table, for instance – the width of the visible plant material on either side should be at least one-and-a-half times the width of the container.

Of course you will not always want to create arrangements that fall into these minimum height or width categories. What about all those times when you just want to arrange a handful of roses in a jug or teapot? A good rule of thumb here is that the visible plant material should never be much less than half the height of the container. Arrange flowers that fall short of that and they seem to be peeping over the rim of the container, like children standing on tiptoe to see over a garden wall!

FLOWER AND LEAF SHAPES

Arranging flowers is rather like working on a jigsaw puzzle: each piece, each flower, leaf and stem, fits happily with its next door neighbours on all sides, and plays its part in contributing to the completed picture. Take one perfect rose away from your finished flower arrangement, and you are left with an awkward gap.

To be sure that every element in your flower design does play its part and fit happily with the others around it, it pays to study the variety of shapes and forms in the floral ingredients. Flowers grow in all shapes and sizes, from rounded, spherical shapes to flat, saucer-like ones; from bell and trumpet shapes like irises, daffodils, and lilies, to umbrella-like domes and soft, fluffy spires. Some flowers, like roses, are full, open, and composed of a multitude of petals; while others, even when fully mature, are tightly furled, revealing little of their inner selves. Some flowers, like hydrangeas, are huge and mop-headed, while others – gypsophila, for example – are so small they appear like tiny specks in an arrangement.

Foliage also comes in a variety of shapes and sizes. Some leaves, such as rosemary and yew, are like sharp little needles along a straight stem; some, like geranium, are round and frilly; others

The flat, round shapes of the marigolds and the deep trumpet shapes of the nasturtiums combine to give 'movement' to the group.

41

– maple, sycamore, and ivy – have a regular 'hand' shape; and still others – sage and ballota – form a dense, almost furry mass. And all that variation makes no mention of their colour. We talk loosely of green foliage, but leaves grow in almost every tint, tone, and shade, from palest cream to rich burgundy, from bright lettuce green to nearly jet black.

Even plant stems have their own individual roles to play. Some – useful for upright designs – are ramrod straight, while others have gently arching curves. Use these natural curves to help you when you want to compose a crescent shape or a 'lazy S' design. Certain stems, like hogweed and wild carrot, fork and branch out from the main upright stem to create interesting geometric patterns; while others – clematis is a good example – are untamable, twisting this way and that and twirling in every direction. Use these convoluted stems to create unusual and interesting outlines and trails.

Once you become aware of the individual shapes and forms of plant material, you will be able to combine two, three, or even more types, each of which brings out the best in the others. An arrangement of round pom-pom dahlias, spherical globe thistles, and onion heads would have little going for it in design terms. All those round flowers and seedheads would look like so many circles drawn on paper, and the arrangement would lack shape and perspective. Equally, a vase of mauve butterfly bush (buddleia), blue *Veronica exaltata*, and purple gayfeather (*Liatris callilepis*) would make a powerful colour impact but a lacklustre design. The almost identical shapes of the flower stems would cancel each other out, and none would capture the attention. By blending fully rounded shapes with trumpet ones and long spires or straight stems of foliage with large fleshy leaves and small clusters, you can create far more depth of interest in your designs, and give every component a share of the limelight.

It is not just a question of which shapes you use, but where you place them in the overall arrangement. The golden rule is that the larger and more substantial the material, whether a dahlia, fig leaf, or centifolia rose, the closer it should go to the centre base of a design; or, in the case of an L-shaped arrangement, to the right angle at the base, where it will become the focal point. Conversely, the more slender and tapering the material, be it a spray of larkspur, a rosemary stem, or a tightly furled daffodil – all known as 'points' – the closer it should go to the edge of the design, where it will form a natural vignette. In-between shapes and sizes, used for the heart of an arrangement, are known as fillers, and can be as varied as tulips, marguerites and carnations.

Sometimes you may have one special flower you want to feature in all its glory. It may be the first or the last precious rose of summer, the only peony you care to cut from the border, or a magnificent poppy. One trick is to surround it with flowers or leaves in its opposing colour on the colour wheel, as discussed in Chapter 1 under the heading *Flower Colours*. Another is to encircle it with plant materials in harmonizing colours, yet widely differing shapes and sizes. A cluster of sweet peas, ranunculus, cornflowers, and scabious, for instance, would make a pretty 'collar' to a full-flowering pink rose, while ensuring the latter captured the limelight.

SELECTING FLOWERS AND FOLIAGE

To ensure your arrangements have the longest possible vase life, it is important to select flowers

A saucer of foam fixed to the rim of the vase transforms it into a pedestal container and facilitates the upright shape of the arrangement.

BOLD STATEMENT

2 The bulbous mushroom shape of the container is complemented by large blooms: a head of blue and green hydrangea and a single orange gerbera. The lilies are clustered together to strengthen their colour impact.

1 An amusing 1940s vase calls for a casual floral arrangement that does not overpower the striking container. The height is set by night-scented stocks and golden lilies held in crumpled wire netting.

YOU WILL NEED

▌ vase

▌ wire-mesh netting

▌ night-scented stocks

▌ lilies

▌ hydrangea

▌ gerbera

▌ irises

▌ daffodils

▌ gypsophila

▌ cornflowers

3 One gnome appears to be supporting a sun-burst arrangement completed by the addition of irises, daffodils and gypsophila. The perennial cornflowers close to the rim of the vase provide a strong colour contrast.

and foliage at the peak of condition. Once flowers have been pollinated and are fully open they begin to fade, and are past their best.

If you have the chance to gather flowers and leaves from the garden or countryside, do so in the morning or evening, at a time when the sun is not fully on them. Choose flowers that are still in the process of maturing. In the case of larkspur and delphinium, for example, this means when only a few florets low down on the stem are fully open, and many of those close to the tip are still in tight bud. Harvest roses when the buds are just beginning to open; if you cut them at the too-tight bud stage they may never fully develop.

Avoid cutting deciduous leaves, and even some evergreens, in early spring when they are at their most attractive bright, light green stage. With the sap still not fully risen in the plants, the young leaves, whether lime, ivy, or yew, will soon wilt and die.

Cut all stems with very sharp stem scissors, secateurs or pruning shears at a very sharp angle, so that you expose the largest possible area of stem tissue. This is the plant's 'mouthpiece', and the greater the area you expose, the more readily the stem will be able to take up water. Particularly in hot weather, it is advisable to take a bucket of water around the garden with you, and place the cut stems in to it straight away.

If you are choosing flowers and foliage from a florist or market stall, similar criteria apply. Look for signs of healthy freshness, and avoid any materials that are fully developed or show signs of wilting or discolouring. Tempting as it

may be to rush home with an armful of golden daffodils, your pleasure, like the flowers themselves, will be short-lived. Also, you will forfeit the joy of watching them gradually unfurl, like a living sculpture.

When you get your plant materials indoors, strip off all the leaves that will come below the water level in an arrangement. Leaves and water do not go well together: they cause the water to discolour and to have a sour odour. Recut all the stems at a sharp angle, preferably under water. This is easy to do if you angle each stem in a wide bowl of water, and it is a great help in preventing the formation of airlocks. Make criss-cross cuts in the base of woody stems – roses, for example – and strip off the bark for about 5cm/2in. This is another way of helping the plant tissue to absorb water. Finally, place all flowers and foliage stems in a bucket of deep water and leave them in a cool, dark place for several hours. This long drink, part of the 'conditioning' process, will greatly extend their eventual vase life. If your flowers have become casualties of a long hot journey, this conditioning treatment should be a life-saver. If it does not revive them, recut the stems once again, and leave them in deep water for another lengthy period. If they *still* look jaded, protect the flower heads by wrapping them in a plastic bag, and stand the stems deep in hot water. Roses, particularly, respond well to this treatment.

Remember there are tight controls on gathering wild plant materials: in the UK it is permissable only to pick rampant weeds and certain very prolific species from public ground, or with the landowner's permission; while in the US, it is illegal to pick wild flowers on any State or national parkland. If you are in any doubt, err on the safe side and do not pick them. Wrap stems in damp tissues as soon as they are cut, and seal the whole stems, including the flowers, into a large plastic bag. The condensation will help to keep often delicate wild materials fresh.

Broom, rosemary, eucalyptus and mahonia leaves, seen dramatically against the light, are arranged on a storage jar of beans.

47

FLOWER CARE

Caring for flowers and foliage as soon as you bring them indoors, and conditioning them to their change of environment, will go a long way towards ensuring they last well once arranged. In addition, there are a few other general guidelines that contribute to a long vase life.

Firstly, the 'vase' itself. It is important that containers and holding materials are kept scrupulously clean. As soon as you dismantle an arrangement, wash and even scrub the container if necessary to remove any water stains and tidemarks. If glass holders show signs of stubborn stains, swirl some raw rice grains around in soapy water. The gentle abrasive action should remove the stains without scratching the container. Wash crumpled wire netting and pick off any stem or leaf pieces adhering to it. And rinse absorbent foam in clean water if you plan to use it again. It may be necessary to cut off a strip that has too many or too-large holes before storing the remainder in airtight conditions.

Make sure there are no leaves or florets below the water line in containers. These are the first cause of souring the water. Check the water each day, and keep the level topped up. This is especially important when using absorbent foam. You must always position it so there is room to pour water over or around it, and it is essential that you check it frequently: if you once allow it to dry out, you cannot make amends.

If flowers wilt with what seems like undue haste – as they may if they were not properly conditioned before arranging, or if they are kept under excessive heat – it is worth recutting the stems and giving them a reviving drink in a large container in a cool place.

You may like to use one of the proprietary brands of flower food, which can help prolong the life of fresh cut flowers. This is often sold as crystals in a convenient sachet form, to be dissolved in a little warm water and then diluted with cold water. You can use it both in 'open' containers and with absorbent foam. If you are using the latter, simply dissolve the crystals in the bowl of water before you soak the foam.

Spraying flowers and foliage with a fine mist of water after arranging them also helps to keep them cool and fresh. In hot weather, particularly, it is a good idea to do this once or twice a day. Remember to remove the arrangement to a draining board or kitchen surface until the water stops dripping.

Heat and light play a significant part in the development of plant materials, and cut flowers are no exception. In general, the cooler and more shady the situation, the longer an arrangement will last. The worst situation for a flower arrangement is a south-facing, sunny window-sill over a radiator; the best, a shady wall in a cool room. If a room has a constant heat source – an all-night burning stove, for instance – it is worth removing an arrangement overnight.

The sad fact is that fresh flowers will eventually die, but you can prolong the life of an arrangement as much as possible by picking or cutting off dead heads regularly. Add extra fresh flowers or leaves to fill in any gaps.

A study in warm shades of pink and red, the arrangement cascades down from a saucer of foam fixed to an openwork vase.

■INDOOR GARDEN

1 The container is a rectangular plastic trough, complete with handle, which is available from some florists. It is just the right size to take a slice cut from a block of foam. The foliage etches in the length of the design and the iris fixes the height.

2 Purple bugle flowers and perennial cornflowers are placed vertically, as if they were growing. The single chrysanthemum at the base, its stem cut very short, represents lawn daisies in a green surround.

3 The completed design is like an indoor flower garden, a herbaceous border packed with contrasting colours, shapes and textures. The broom and the variegated periwinkle visually lighten the base.

YOU WILL NEED

▪ rectangular plastic trough

▪ foam

▪ ivy

▪ cypress foliage

▪ bugle flowers

▪ cornflowers

▪ spray chrysanthemums

▪ broom

▪ variegated periwinkle

▪ irises

▪ pansies

CHAPTER THREE

FLOWERS
FOR
EVERY DAY

Arranging flowers around the home should not be considered a special task reserved for holidays and when visitors are expected. Indeed, a few flowers are just what it takes to give your spirits a welcome lift any day of the week. What could be more cheerful than waking up to the morning light streaming on to a vase of flowers on the bedroom window-sill, or a jug of casually arranged flowers on the breakfast table. And as you come home from work or grocery shopping, a vase of colourful flowers in the hallway, or a pot of plants hanging on a wall bracket spells out a special welcome.

Simplicity at its most charming: a metal pot of wild roses and strawberry flowers.

It might be a council of perfection to have flowers in every area of the home, though dining and sitting or living room, hallway and bedroom, kitchen and bathroom all look more cosy and relaxing for the addition of a floral group, however simple. Consider the special needs of each separate area, and you might decide to arrange some flowers in each one, in turn.

DINING ROOM

If the dining room is in only occasional use, it is a good idea to have a small dried flower arrangement on the table, and perhaps one on a side table, too. Then, whenever you open the door, the room looks lived in and welcoming.

The dining table is the usual focus of attention, and a perfect situation for a fresh flower arrangement. As the display will be viewed from all sides, it has to be what is called an 'all-round' design, or one that is equally attractive from all angles. This necessitates turning the arrangement around as you compose it. Some arrangers like to place the flower container on a cake-icing turntable, and give it a quarter turn as they work.

Dining-table designs should be in proportion to the table. While circular designs such as domes and low pyramids look well on a round table and oblong ones such as elongated triangles look tailor-made for a rectangular one, there is no need to stick rigidly to those patterns. The proportion of the design is more significant than the shape. When entertaining, height is an important factor, and a design should never be so tall that it obscures the view – and inhibits the conversation – across the table.

Simple containers are best for everyday arrangements. A piece of spare china from the table setting or a container that picks up a single colour in the china pattern would harmonize well. Glass adds sparkle to a dining table, and is always a good choice.

A group of straight-sided tumblers close together – especially effective if they are of different heights – looks attractive, whether filled with similar, harmonizing, or contrasting flowers. Pink, yellow, and white roses in each of the containers; forget-me-nots in one, pansies in another, and anemones in the third; or a handful of flowering herbs in each – whatever your choice, this quick and easy-to-arrange group will command attention. In place of glasses you could use specimen vases, decorative glass jars, or old medicine or drinks bottles. Placing a single flower in each of three or five decorative porcelain or glass bottles (odd numbers always look best) maximizes the display value of a minimum number of stems.

For a country look, a trio of small baskets – the kind you can buy cheaply in charity shops or jumble sales – looks pretty when spilling over with trailing leaves and tiny flowers. Group them in a cluster on a round table, in a staggered line on a long one. If you do have a long and narrow table, remember the people at either end. They can feel quite deprived if there is only a small solitary arrangement at the centre. A group of three containers, or a small arrangement in, say, a spice jar at each place setting can bring them right into the party!

Floating flowers look pretty for a dining-table setting, and here's another design that is assembled in moments. Choose your most attractive glass bowl, china dish, or a collection of chubby glasses, and float a few leaves and flowerheads in clear, sparkling water or in water coloured with one or two drops of food colouring. Spider chrysanthemums are a good choice since

For afternoon tea in the garden, a high-profile arrangement that includes luscious, ripe strawberries speared on wooden cocktail sticks.

1 A strip of florists' clay secures the plastic saucer to the hand-thrown pottery plate. The graceful lines of the snowdrop leaves, forming an inverted 'T' shape, are followed by the contrastingly spiky and reddish-brown berberis stems.

◼ COLOUR BALANCE

2 The three gerberas, each one facing a different way, distribute their bright colour evenly throughout the design. A trio of crimson carnations forms the centre of the group and provides both shape and colour contrast.

YOU WILL NEED

- pottery plate
- plastic saucer
- florists' clay
- cylinder of foam

- snowdrop leaves
- berberis stems
- gerberas
- carnations
- hawthorn sprays
- sage leaves
- lamium leaves

3 Crimson spray carnations accentuate the basic shape of the arrangement and perfectly match their larger counterparts. Sprays of hawthorn buds and purple sage leaves fill in the centre of this strikingly modern display.

they have a proven pedigree: they are the flowers most often used in this way in China, where the practice originated. Place the containers on the table, wait until the water is absolutely still, then gently lower in the plant materials, using a cocktail stick to position them.

Make a circle of leaves to form a 'collar' around a single floating flower, or arrange a random or geometric pattern of flowers and foliage. Other flowers that take well to the water are fully opened roses, camellias, delphinium florets, and carnations. Large trumpet and barrel-shaped flowers, like mallow and tulips, and very delicate ones tend to capsize.

For a special occasion, add floating nightlights – ordinary ones sink; you have to buy the special ones – and alternate them with the flowers. It's the quickest, easiest way ever to decorate the table for an impromptu supper party, and another idea you can carry out with style with very few flowers.

The Victorians loved shallow arrangements for the centre of the table. A favourite in those days was a leaf posy composed, according to size, on a flat dish, plate, or saucer. It's a pretty idea to copy, and one that is sure to be a talking point. Collect a handful of different foliage shapes with as much colour variation as possible. There could be red radiccio leaves, frilly lettuce or ornamental cabbage, maple, chestnut, spotted laurel, ivy, geranium, any fallen leaves – use whatever you have and what you can find. Arrange a ring of the largest leaves around the outside of the container, partly cover it with a ring of smaller, contrasting leaves, and then another, until the dish is covered through to the centre. Finish with a single flower or a piece of fruit in the middle, and spray fresh (not dried) leaves with a fine mist of water to help prolong their moistureless 'vase' life.

A covering of leaves or moss makes a natural background for a simulated indoor garden, with an arrangement of flowers appearing to grow from

One perfect full-blown pink rose, surrounded by smaller blooms, becomes the focal point of this informal table-top design.

59

▮JEWEL BOX

1 The small lidded wicker basket is lined with plastic to make it moisture-proof. The block of foam extends above the rim so that the stems may be slanted downwards over the container.

2 Lilies-of-the-valley follow the lines of the sweet pea stems. The five coral and saffron-striped pinks are placed so that their colour is evenly distributed throughout the design.

▬ YOU WILL NEED

▌ small, lidded wicker basket

▌ plastic, for lining

▌ block of foam

▌ cocktail sticks (to prop up lid)

▌ sweet peas

▌ lilies-of-the-valley

▌ pinks

▌ foliage

3 Pastel pink sweet peas
and border pinks fill in the
design and form a colour link
between the white and the
coral. A few sprays of leaves
add shape definition.

the container. Choose a shallow, straight-sided dish or a straight-sided basket, fitted with an inner liner, in proportion to your table. Line the container with a slice of soaked absorbent foam, and cover it with a thick layer of leaves or moss. Short-stemmed sprays of ivy nestling against the foam, or clumps of damp sphagnum moss held in place with bent wires or U-shaped hairpins, give a 'carpet of green' effect. Then press sturdy flower stems, well apart, through into the foam so that the design looks like a nature garden. Tulips towering over primulas; narcissi standing proud above grape hyacinths; Icelandic poppies with cornflowers – try mixing and matching two contrasting flower types of different sizes in this unusual way.

Flowers and fruit make a lovely partnership for the dining table, and one that can be as simple as you wish. You could, for example, arrange a pyramid of green apples on a dish lined with ivy leaves and simply tuck a few fresh or dried flowers among them. (Remember to give fresh flowers a good, long drink of water beforehand.) Or arrange a dish of red, crimson, and purple plums, and tuck in sprays of the brightest rosehips and shiniest elderberries you can find.

For a long-lasting arrangement, partially wrap small blocks of soaked foam in kitchen foil, to prevent moisture seepage, and bury them, (or water-filled egg cups or spice jars) between the pieces of fruit. That gives you the chance to arrange one or two showy flowers like double poppies or alstroemeria (Peruvian lilies) or small bunches of mixed flowers, such as a nosegay of spray carnations, marguerites, miniature roses, and trailing variegated ivy.

For a special effect, and one that makes an excellent winter table decoration, you can use pieces of fruit as the flower containers. Arrange a bowl of zingy citrus fruits or mixed fruits, including a pineapple and trailing grapes, and mingle them with scooped-out lemon and orange shells fitted with inner containers. Fill the shells with tiny flowers and leaves for the sparkiest centrepiece ever. Instructions for fruit containers are given in Chapter 2 under the heading *Choosing Containers*.

CANDLE POWER

It doesn't have to be a super-special occasion to merit candles on the table. Some of the slow-burning types are deceptively economical, and what meal isn't made all the more festive for their cheery glow? Fat, stubby candles look good on saucers when surrounded by a few dried flowerheads, or arranged with fruit and flowers on a flat dish. Polish the fruit before arranging it, and you really will be able to see your face in it! Or press one, two, or three tall, slender candles into absorbent foam, according to its size, before arranging flowers. To avoid breaking up the foam you can buy candle spikes, green plastic pointed spikes with a cylindrical hole, about 2cm/¾in across, just the size to take a standard candle. They are especially useful when you want to arrange flowers and foliage or leaves and berries in a pre-formed plastic ring, as you do when making an Advent candle ring (see the project in Chapter 4, pages 82 and 83).

Candles can be used not just as accessories, but as 'flower holders', too. It's a charming idea to bind fresh or dried flowers around tall straight candles, and one that makes a party table really

Sweet peas and roses are arranged in a pyramid shape, an 'all-round' style for the centre of a table.

come to life. Take a handful of small flowers in a
colour-matching theme. There may be pink
and yellow freesias, spray carnations, primulas,
and snippings of gypsophila. Give the flowers a
long drink, and hold them low down against the
candle. Bind the stems in place, a ring of flowers
all around the candle, with fine silver roll wire or
fuse wire. Stand the candles in sturdy holders,
and keep an eye on them as they burn down:
don't allow the flame to get too close to the
flowers, especially if you use dried ones.

Consider the aroma of flowers before making
your final choice for the dining table. A few
scented freesias, a few sprigs of herbs, or a
cluster of violets will all contribute a subtle
aroma that lends an air of luxury to a room. The
golden rule, though, is not to overdo it. A pot of
hyacinths on the dining table might look pretty as
a picture, but their pervasive smell, however
pleasant in another setting, would completely
overpower the mingled flavours of the food.

This brings up a point, however: pots of
flowering plants do look pretty as a picture on the
table. If you haven't time to buy flowers, if the
shops are closed, or if you simply want an instant
decoration, gather up three or four small potted
plants from around the home. Stand them, if
possible, in matching or harmonizing containers,
and arrange them in a cluster or jagged line along
the table centre. Pink and white cyclamen, pink
and red primulas, red azaleas – they make an
eye-catching group in no time at all.

If foliage plants rather than flowering ones are
your forte, why not bring these on to the table
now and again? Group several contrasting plants
together, choosing them for their variety of leaf
shape, texture, and colour. They can look
stunning. If you are not entirely happy with the
effect or want to add a little more colour, you may
be able to supplement the group with a jar of
flowers – just a handful of daffodils, perhaps –
standing among them, or cheat nature and 'plant'
a few flower stems temporarily in the flower pots.

A few freesias blended with
spray carnations and zinnias
give a hint of an aroma in a
design for a formal table
setting.

1 The plastic saucer holding the foam cylinder is firmly fixed to the rim of the coffee pot with a ring of florists' clay. The roses and geranium are positioned to form a lop-sided fan shape.

■ PINK PERFECTION

2 Sprays of silver-green and aromatic leaves, some with their stems cut very short, fill in the spaces between the flowers and provide a natural background.

▬ YOU WILL NEED

- ■ coffee pot, or similar
- ■ plastic saucer
- ■ cylinder of foam
- ■ florists' clay

- ▌roses
- ▌geranium flower
- ▌silver-green foliage
- ▌sweet peas
- ▌pinks

3 The sweet peas exactly match the colour of the roses, but their shape provides an interesting contrast. The pinks, close to the centre and the base of the design, add a striking depth of colour.

For a more varied look, and if there's room in the flower pot, sink a small water holder or a piece of soaked, foil-wrapped foam into the soil, and arrange a cascade of flowers beside the plant. The dense foliage of your chosen plant will perfectly complement the flowers in this impromptu *pot et fleur*.

But, in flower-arrangement terms, there is more to a dining room than just the table. There may be a side table, a sideboard, a window table, or a cupboard where another flower arrangement, a less personal one, is appropriate. Choose plant materials that will blend with those in the table design. The arrangements may be of a completely different shape and scale, but they should have a visual link. You may have a rounded dome of pale pink and cream freesias and alstroemeria on the table, a design arranged in concentric circles like a Victorian posy. This style may be out of proportion on a sideboard, but you could echo the colours or repeat one of the feature flowers. An arrangement in deeper shades of pink and yellow may be just what's called for; or one that majors on alstroemeria, combining the lilies with other larger blooms.

Consider the background against which the 'second' flower arrangement will be seen. Is the wallcovering plain or fancy; geometric or fussy; brightly coloured or neutral? Take this into account when planning the arrangement, and choose flowers and foliage that will both complement the background and yet be clearly seen against it. It may be that a design in an urn-shaped vase would benefit from having an edging of substantial stems of foliage to separate it, visually, from an intricate pattern. Or it may be that only an arrangement composed of large flowers and leaves has any chance of competing with a small floral wallpaper pattern.

The siting of dining-room arrangements needs consideration. It's a good idea to position a design where it will be the first focus of attention as people come in to a room, or where it can be easily seen and admired by people seated at the table. A long, low design on a low table behind the door breaks all the rules about maximizing on visibility.

THE SITTING OR LIVING ROOM

Similar criteria apply to flower arrangements for a sitting or living room. Remember that, as always, the flowers should give the maximum possible pleasure to everyone in the room. This could best be achieved, perhaps, by placing a small arrangement close to each seating area. A jug of roses on a side table beside a favourite chair, a circlet of tiny blooms in a posy ring on a coffee table, and a romantic collection of misty-blue flowers beside a window seat might be all it takes for every member of the family or every guest to feel special and cosseted.

Make sure containers placed on wine tables, especially spindly ones, are sturdy enough to withstand knocks from children and pets, and that coffee-table designs are of the kind that really look best when viewed from above. Domes, shallow pyramids, and irregular 'all-round' designs are all suitable for this purpose. A cylinder of foam held by a prong on a plate or saucer is a good foundation for any of these shapes. Keep coffee-table arrangements neat and compact so they do not intrude too much on the useable space.

It may be that a room corner is the ideal place for a larger feature arrangement, the kind that stands on a tall table and can be admired above the seating level. Consider the light factor, and choose flower colours accordingly. If any room

A fireplace in summer remains a focal point in the room. Here it is decorated with a pot of peonies, sweet williams, and roses.

corner is underlit and inclined to be gloomy, keep flower colours light; deep reds, blues, mauves, and bronzes will fade into obscurity and only compound the problem. Among dried flowers, honesty and helichrysums are the most reflective, catching and returning every shaft of available light. Choose the palest tints of the everlasting flowers, such as cream, yellow, peach, and apricot, with a few deeper shades recessed into the arrangement to give it depth and perspective. This means arranging the darker flowers first, cutting the stems short so they nestle closest to the holding material or the heart of the design. Then the lighter colours can thrust upwards and outwards, shining like miniature beacons throughout the arrangement.

Whenever the light factor is low, pale colours are the order of the day for fresh flowers, too. Choosing flowers and foliage that have a high gloss factor – tulips, lilies, and ranunculus; laurel, elaeagnus, and variegated ivy – considerably aids visibility. Pale colours and shiny materials continue to glow as dusk falls, and can light up a corner as effectively as switching on a lamp.

The fireplace is usually one of the main focal points of a room, whether or not a fire is lit. Whenever the hearth is not in use, however, a flower arrangement or a collection of plants can take over the visual role. Indeed, you can practise illusory tactics by arranging flowers in dancing-flame colours of red, orange, blue, and gold, and make believe there's a warm glow.

Consider the fireplace opening as an arch or a frame, according to its shape, and it's a natural background for flower arrangements. Consider the colours and the texture, too, and choose flowers that will look well against them. If the fireplace has a dark surround, vibrant colours will look more than usually dramatic, and could dominate the room. Pale pastels would look more than ever cool; too cool and ethereal, perhaps, as winter approaches.

Choose containers that are in proportion to the recess – large enough not to be dwarfed by the opening – and that look good at ground level. Willow baskets with either side or up-and-over handles, paint-sprayed 'fashion' baskets, preserving pans, large casseroles, wooden boxes, and garden trugs would all be appropriate. A collection of stone or earthenware pickle jars filled with branches and flowers, a trio of substantial jugs, a group of potted plants: there are limitless ways of bridging the fireplace gap.

Since the fireplace is likely to be resting from its function for weeks or months on end, it is a good idea to consider a long-lasting arrangement of dried flowers so that, once in place, it becomes part of the furnishings throughout the summer. Make up a selection of dried and preserved materials to include oats, wheat, glycerined foliage, helichrysums, tansy, and achillea, and it need not cost the earth. Give pride of place in the centre of the design to more costly flowers, such as dried rosebuds and luxuriant peonies.

If yours is a Victorian fireplace with a small opening and a high fire basket, you could turn back the clock and simulate a popular Victorian flower-arranging theme, the cornucopia. To do this, fix a round container into the opening and fit it firmly with dry holding foam. Then arrange dried flowers to spill forwards, pouring out of the container as it if were a horn of plenty. And if your local craft shop has one in stock, you can carry out the theme to perfection: fix a corn-dolly cornucopia into the opening and have it overflowing with grains, grasses, and colourful dried flowers.

Harvest plaits at the side of a fireplace add a charmingly rustic touch, and can be left permanently in place. Buy ready-made raffia plaits (market stalls and florists have them), and decorate them with nuts and cones, heads of sweetcorn or hops, textured seedheads, and dried flowers. To attach cones and nuts, wrap a

A pair of baskets can be used to dramatic effect, one for a bright collection of garden flowers, the other for highly polished fruit.

1 A casserole dish fitted in the craggy basket holds a block of soaked foam which is almost concealed by the sprays of glossy hypericum foliage. The three irises define the height and width of the design.

■ BREATH OF SPRING

2 Golden daffodils begin to fill in the design. If their stems are too soft and pliable to press into the foam it may be necessary to strengthen them by pushing in a medium-gauge stub wire.

YOU WILL NEED

- ▮ basket
- ▮ waterproof container
- ▮ block of foam
- ▮ plastic prong
- ▮ florists' clay

- ▮ hypericum foliage
- ▮ daffodils
- ▮ irises

3 The completed shape – a host of golden daffodils contrasted with a handful of golden and white irises. This arrangement would be especially suitable to stand in a hearth or room corner.

piece of wire around the middle, twist the two ends together to form a stem, and push it into the depth of the plait.

WINDOW DRESSING

Windows are often the main or, after the fireplace, secondary focal points in a room, and window-sill arrangements have a special role to play. They, too, are seen in the context of a frame, and should not be so small that they pale into insignificance. The ratio of arrangement to window size may well be determined by the quality of the outlook. A medium-sized arrangement placed to one side – say an enamel jug of pink and white lilac and anemones – can draw attention to the window and lead the eye to the view beyond. If, on the other hand, the view is not the strong point (the window may look on to a wall, a shed, or a roofline in all-too-close proximity), then a flower arrangement can cheerfully mask or obscure it. You might choose to arrange a large jug – glass is especially effective – of translucent leaves such as lime or sycamore to make believe there's a tree right outside the window. You could arrange a pot of cow parsley and campion flowers, the wide-spreading white umbellifers acting like a lace curtain in filtering the view. Or, for a more permanent decoration, you might like to compose a jug of dried flowers, including honesty, white pearl everlasting, and shiny acroclinium.

Another way of treating a window when the view is not to your advantage is to hang dried flowers and herbs from a cord stretched from side to side of the frame. They make a wonderful pelmet at whatever level you choose.

South-facing and sunny windows are a problem, because strong light and heat hastens the development (and consequently shortens the life) of fresh flowers, and causes dried ones to fade. If you do decide to place flowers in this situation, try to remove them during the heat of the day, or screen them with a curtain or blind.

However you choose to arrange flowers for a window-sill, remember that windows have eyes and people approaching your home may see the reverse of the design first. If you compose a lovely arrangement in, say, a narrow-necked vase fitted with green stem-holding foam, make sure to finish off the back so it looks as neat, though not necessarily as colourful, as the front. This means covering the back of the foam with short sprays of foliage or large individual leaves and a few second-best flowers so it cannot be seen from any angle. New enthusiasts to flower arranging often omit this finishing touch, and wonder why their designs look flat and one-dimensional, lacking depth and perspective. Even when composing an arrangement that is to stand against a wall, it is important to pretend it can be seen from the back, and give it this essential degree of extra care.

THE HALLWAY

Flower arrangements for a hallway, welcoming as those on a window-sill, have a unique feature. Unlike those in any of the living rooms, they are seen and admired only in passing. This means they can be more strident, more assertive, more dominant than arrangements elsewhere in the home, which you have to live with for hours on end. The hallway is the ideal place, therefore, to try out colour splashes and clashes, and way-out and wild-looking styles. It may even take designs with one or more of these qualities to stop the family in their tracks as they rush in and out.

A jug of wheat and a maize doll, a rustic way to mask an uninspiring view from a bedroom window.

If there's no space in the hall for a table, perhaps you can arrange a dried or fresh flower group for the window-sill; have a shell-shaped wall vase tumbling over with trailing preserved leaves and dried flowers; have an arrangement spilling over from a shelf unit, or a ball of dried flowers (see Chapter 5) hanging over the stairs. The hallway hasn't been designed yet in which there is no space at all for flowers!

FLOWERS FOR THE BEDROOM, KITCHEN AND BATHROOM

In complete contrast to those for a hallway, flower arrangements for a bedroom or guest room should be easy on the eye and composed in restful colours. Tints and shades of blue, mauve, and green, and all pastels, are considered most relaxing. Think what effect you want the flowers to create. Does a flower design need to provide a pool of colour or create a cool spot; does it need to harmonize with the furnishings, or would a contrast be more effective? Answer those questions and you can decide what colour groups would be most flattering to the room, whether it would be a bowl of blue, mauve, pink and yellow pansies and anemones or a bunch of all-white gypsophila; a specimen vase draped with deep purple and white fuschias or a pot of delphinium and roses. Place some flowers where shafts of morning light will strike them, and others, in an act of pure self-indulgence, on your dressing-table. If there is a mirror on the furniture, check the back view of the arrangement for its interest value, and also for tell-tale signs of stem-holding foam or crushed wire. There is nothing at all romantic about even a peep of the mechanics that keep the flowers so prettily in place.

Avoid heavily-scented flowers in a bedroom for a practical reason: some people find they give them a headache.

A flower arrangement in the kitchen can have a relaxing effect, too, toning down the intensely utilitarian aspect of the room. Consider using containers that look entirely appropriate there – clean food and drink cans (some of which have strikingly attractive and graphic designs), striped kitchenware jugs, flowerpots with inner liners, enamel coffee pots, tea pots, milk cans and wooden containers such as flour bins and salt boxes. Create compact designs that will not get in the way, and use long-lasting flowers such as daisy chrysanthemums, marigolds, marguerites, zinnias, pinks, carnations, tulips, and daffodils. Grains, grasses, and dried everlasting flowers are a good kitchen choice, too. A wooden tub of dried wheat speckled with bright red helichrysums lends a country look reminiscent of a field of poppies. A red-and-white Coke can of red and white tulips is quite an eye-opener in the early morning, while a flower pot simply filled with a heavy bunch of marigolds in appropriately marmalade colours makes an attractive breakfast-time display.

Plan to keep a few fresh herbs growing in pots on the window-sill and, failing any flowers, you have an instant decoration for the kitchen table. If you have fresh herbs in the garden, there is nothing more suitable for a kitchen arrangement. A honey pot filled with young leaves of sage and purple sage, marjoram, mint, lemon balm, and golden thyme, provides both decoration and culinary ingredients. Later in the season when herbs go to seed, a tall preserving jar of fennel or dill seedheads looks equally good in the kitchen or on a sunny living-room window-sill.

Bathrooms, like kitchens, are subject to rapid temperature and humidity changes, and so the most good-tempered and long-lasting flowers are most suitable here, too. Among the dried flowers, honesty and Chinese lanterns and everlastings such as helichrysums, acrocliniums, rhodanthe and statice are least likely to reabsorb moisture in the form of steam and therefore unlikely to be subject to mould. Delicate, papery dried flowers such as larkspur, peonies, and

rosebuds are best reserved for more equable climes around the home.

Clear glass containers look especially good in a bathroom, and you can choose ones as varied as sturdy tumblers and goldfish bowls, cosmetic bottles, and rectangular troughs. If you need to use stem-holding materials in wide containers, this is the ideal place to feature glass marbles, pebbles, granite chippings, or clear or coloured plastic 'ice cubes', which all look attractive in a watery context. Large shells fitted with soaked foam and arranged with trailing flowers make a good window-sill design; or use the containers to make a more permanent display by planting them with trailing plants such as tradescantia (spiderwort) and mind-your-own-business. Shells make pretty bathroom accessories, too. Place one or two beside a window-sill or shelf arrangement, and – in the shell-equals-pearl context – tie an old pearl bead necklace around the neck of a plain container such as a glass jar or a creamware pot. It makes all the difference between an everyday arrangement and an inspired one.

Foliage plants can give a bathroom a look of luxury. A group of plants arranged in a wide basket or a large washstand bowl makes a lovely floor-standing display and one that will thrive indefinitely. Be sure to check the instruction labels of plants before you buy to ensure they will take well to hot and steamy conditions. Weeping fig, scented pelargonium, ivy, and African violets are just a few among many that would turn your bathroom into a verdant hothouse.

A hollowed-out and re-baked puff-shaped loaf makes an appropriate container for a kitchen table. Here it is arranged with coral and orange carnations and marigolds.

CASCADE OF LEAVES

1 The saucer of foam is fixed to the vase with a band of florists' clay. Ornamental cabbage, rosemary, poppy, lamium and hosta leaves, with all their colour contrasts, begin to etch in the outlines of the arrangement.

2 Trails of ivy at the sides sweep down almost to the table top, and attractively enclose the vase. Short sprays of silver-leafed curry plant are silhouetted against the deep purple cabbage leaves.

3 The medley of foliage now includes hollyhock, aquilegia, hypericum, periwinkle and fennel, with the slim arching lines of pampas grass cascading over at each side.

YOU WILL NEED

▌vase

▌plastic saucer

▌cylinder of foam

▌florists' clay

▌ornamental cabbage

▌rosemary leaves

▌poppy leaves

▌lamium leaves

▌hosta leaves

▌hollyhock leaves

▌aquilegia foliage

▌hypericum foliage

▌periwinkle foliage

▌fennel leaves

▌pampas grass leaves

▌ivy

CHAPTER FOUR

FLOWERS FOR SPECIAL OCCASIONS

Flowers and foliage are in the front line of the decoration scene whenever there's a celebration in the air. Since the earliest times people have decked their places of worship, their homes, and even themselves with flowers for festivals and special family occasions. And flowers have long been recognized as the most personal and cherished of gifts to express happiness and condolence, affection and gratitude. A glorious display of fruit and flowers arranged in church for the harvest festival; a welcome ring of evergreens on the front door to greet visitors at Christmas time; a nosegay of flowers as a token of affection on Mother's Day; a presentation posy for a visiting speaker at a public function – holidays and red-letter days of every kind are all the more enjoyable for the special joy that flowers bring.

A circlet of dried grasses studded with colourful flowers makes a dramatic wall decoration for a harvest-time party.

1 The foam in the pre-formed ring (available from some florists) is soaked to capacity. The candles are held in plastic candle spikes which pierce the foam without breaking it or creating large holes.

YOU WILL NEED

▐ pre-formed foam ring
▐ plastic candle spikes
▐ candles

▐ yew foliage
▐ cypress foliage
▐ juniper foliage
▐ holly sprigs
▐ ivy
▐ helichrysum flowers

2 Short-cut sprays of mixed evergreen foliage – yew, cypress, juniper, holly and ivy – form the basis of the ring. Care must be taken to cover both the inside and outside surfaces of the plastic casing.

■ ADVENT RING

3 The Advent ring glows in the light of four candles, traditionally lighted one in each week before Christmas. The design is finished with cream, pink and crimson helichrysum flowers nestling among the foliage.

All these and many other special occasions offer you a golden opportunity to adapt your own personal style of arranging flowers in a way that will give pleasure to others. Just because the occasion *is* special, and the flowers may be on view to a wider than usual audience, does not mean that you have to adopt an unfamiliar or formal style far removed from your own preference. Indeed, flowers arranged naturally and with no apparent conformity to a rule book bring a welcome personal touch to any event.

Whenever you are asked to arrange flowers in a church, a hall, or another large public place, there are only two rules to follow. Rule one is never on any account to be overawed by the scale of the building or the importance of the occasion. And rule two is to plan the flower arrangements with meticulous care at every stage. Once you have taken accurate measurements at the site, made rough sketches of your ideas for the designs, and made a list of the 'ingredients' you will need, the job seems half done.

For your own peace of mind, do the initial planning as soon as possible. Ask for permission to visit the building, and assess the best places for flower arrangements: where they will be most readily seen by the largest number of people, or where they will create an 'intimate' setting for the participants – for example, at the altar for a wedding, and close to the font for a christening.

In a church, check whether there are any restrictions on flower placements – some churchmen do not allow flowers on the font – and if there are any resident containers you can use. Most churches have at least one or two pedestals and other large containers, which are regularly used. And, as a matter of courtesy, check with the rota organizer that you may take over the flower duty at the specified time.

Study the background to your chosen sites, whether it is plain plaster, the geometric outlines of brick, mellow stone, carved wood, or a patterned fabric. This will help you to decide how clearly defined the floral outlines need to be in order to stand out from the surface behind them. Measure any niches or alcoves, the width of the window-sills and pew ends, the size of a chest or table and any other relevant features, so you can plan designs that will be in scale and proportion. Take note, too, of the size and aspect of the windows that will have a bearing on your choice of flowers. If, for instance, an arrangement is to be placed in a darkish area of the building, this disadvantage can be largely overcome by choosing white and pastel-coloured flowers and variegated foliage. If, on the other hand, some designs are likely to be in full sunlight, medium tones would be a better choice. In the full glare of strong light, pale tints tend to burn out and appear drained of all their colour, while dark shades – and especially dark evergreen leaves – appear darker still, and may even take on a sombre look.

Planning the designs in detail is one of the most rewarding aspects of the task. You might decide to have a pair of pedestals, one at either side of a door or at the altar steps. Think of these as no more than side-table designs placed on a slender stand, and they lose some of their undeserved mystique. Remember: because of those slender stands, pedestals need secure groundwork, a real heavy-duty job of securing the foam to the container to the stand. Remember, too, that a pair of pedestals must match exactly. Symmetrical designs make this easier to achieve; asymmetrical designs must be worked in reverse, each one a mirror-image of the other.

Bright pink gerberas and campion are veiled by sheep's parsley and gypsophila in an arrangement for an outdoor party.

84

■ HANGING BASKET

1 The basket is lined with a sheet of plastic to retain the moisture from one-and-a-half blocks of soaked foam. The copper beech leaves spilling over at each side and reaching up to the handle, define the graceful shape of the design.

2 Sprays of bronze and orange spray chrysanthemums tone perfectly with the golden lilies and apricot carnations and give the design a look of abundance.

■

YOU WILL NEED

- ▌hanging wall basket
- ▌plastic for lining
- ▌1½ blocks of foam

- ▌copper beech leaves
- ▌spray chrysanthemums
- ▌lilies
- ▌carnations
- ▌spray carnations

3 Small colour highlights in the completed design are provided by the clutch of coral spray carnations. This arrangement would be suitable for a harvest festival or to set the scene for an autumn wedding in the country.

Window-sill arrangements can be L-shaped to define a corner or long, low horizontals trailing prettily over the sill. It is customary to arrange church flowers in containers that will ultimately be concealed by the natural materials, so discarded utensils such as old baking tins and dishes would be ideal. If you are worried there might be some tell-tale show-through, a coat of paint to tone with the background is all that is needed. Containers do not have to be unseen, however, and casually arranged jugs or vases could be used to good effect instead. For a harvest festival, a jug of wheat and an arrangement of fruit and preserves glowing golden against the light makes a dramatic still-life display in a window.

For a wedding, arrangements on the pew ends create a delightful floral avenue for the bridal couple. To make them, you can use small blocks of soaked foam wrapped in foil for moisture protection, or the smallest size of pre-formed plastic and foam rings, available from florists. One type of plastic holder, just the right size to take a thin slice cut from a foam block, comes complete with a handle and is ideal to hang vertically. Another possibility is a foam ball. Soak it in water, cut it in half, wrap it in foil, insert a wire hanging hook, and you have the base for two dome-shaped pew-end designs.

Whether your planned designs are curvy triangular shapes for pedestals or cascades for pew ends, it is helpful to make rough colour sketches. Use crayons or felt-tipped pens and you can create, however roughly, a visual impression of not only the outline but the colour balance as well. Draw in the outline materials, the fillers and the central features to represent the focal points, and use the sketches to calculate the quantity of flowers and foliage needed.

Prepare as many containers as possible at home. Where this is not practicable, arrange to complete them in advance of the occasion. Condition all the materials thoroughly overnight

and then, on the day, take your travelling flower arranger's kit of plastic sheeting and newspaper to cover the floor, a cloth to mop up any spills, secateurs or pruning shears, medium-gauge stub wires to reinforce any droopy stems – tulips, for example – and a water mister to give the flowers a last-minute shower. In hot weather, spray flowers over and over again to keep them looking their radiant best.

A GIFT OF FLOWERS

Arranging flowers for a gift is one of the most delightful and rewarding aspects of the craft, and one that has many design possibilities. You might decide to give a casually arranged posy composed in the hand, one with all the innocent charm of a child's first bunch of flowers. Choose at least two flower types so the posy has rhythm and variety. There might be boldly coloured ranunculus arranged among a cloud of gypsophila which gives a pretty veiling effect and slightly softens the impact of the bright tones; there could be multicoloured primula arranged with fragrant paper-white narcissi; or garden marigolds and bright yellow golden rod for a real burst of sunshine. Whatever your selection, choose flowers with complementary colours and contrasting shapes so your posy has form and shape. Include a spray or two of leaves if possible: not only is it traditional to do so, but foliage helps protect the flowers in transit.

A sheaf of flowers may be thought of as a simple posy on a larger scale. You might have the chance to pick flowers from a garden, or make a selection from a florist to compose the design

Fresh flowers wired on to a twig ring make a pretty design for a family service in church. This one was for a christening.

CHRISTMAS SPIRIT

1 You could convert a plain basket by wiring on rows of fir cones until it is completely covered; or make just one row under the rim. The basket is fitted with a plastic saucer and a foam cylinder.

2 Sprays of juniper and holly are built up to cover the foam and form a rounded dome shape. The crimson carnations appear at their brightest when they are set among contrasting green.

YOU WILL NEED

▌ basket

▌ plastic saucer

▌ cylinder of foam

▌ juniper foliage

▌ holly

▌ carnations

▌ ivy

3 The simple basket arrangement would make a striking table centre design for Christmas. With its abundance of foliage it would also make a welcome gift for a friend who does not have access to a garden.

yourself. If you know the recipient's tastes, choose colours that will harmonize with her home colour schemes, or ones that happen to be her favourites. If this is not possible – as in the case of a visiting speaker, for example – play safe and choose medium tones. Peaches and cream or the softest pinks and blues are surer choices than a strident blend of, say, red and yellow.

Sheafs of flowers are easiest to compose on a table. Place a covering of leaves – there may be ferns or fennel, beech or birch – to make a fan shape. The foliage will both frame and protect the flowers. Then place a few of the longest-stemmed flowers (daisy chrysanthemums, michaelmas daisies, mimosa, statice) to reach almost to the tip of the leaves. Arrange more flowers in layers, the stems getting progressively shorter, until the shortest ones – maybe partly opened roses or shapely anemones – are close to the handle. Bind the stems with raffia or fine twine, and tie them with a ribbon bow.

A pretty addition to the floral scene, and one that makes delightful presentation bows, is raffia paper ribbon, sold by the metre or yard in a tightly rolled rope. You simply unravel it to its full width (about 10cm/4in), cut it to the width you require, and tie it with a flourish.

Fragrant flowers evoke all the joy of a garden on a summer's evening, and add immeasurably to the pleasure of a gift. Bear this in mind when choosing presentation flowers, and try to include at least one flower or foliage type that has a distinctive aroma. There may be narcissi, freesia or lavender or, among the fragrant leaves, lemon balm, rosemary, marjoram, or lemon-scented pelargonium. Just brushing against the posy releases the scent, and adds a delightful dimension to the design.

It was the Victorians who perfected the state of the art in posy design, composing meaningful collections of flowers and leaves within strictly formal outlines. The classic Victorian posy is made up of concentric ring after ring of flowers

arranged around a central bloom, usually a tightly furled rose bud, and protected by a collar of leaves. For good measure and romantic contrast, the posies often had another layer, an outer ring of frilled cotton, pleated lace, or a crisp paper doily.

Such posies are composed in the hand, then gently rearranged until there isn't a flower or a leaf out of place. To achieve this, hold the central flower firmly, arrange a ring of flowers around it and then, when they have formed a neat circle, continue with the next band and the next. Your choice of flowers will depend on just how prim and proper you want your posy to seem. Compact blooms such as spray carnations, cornflowers, rosebuds, and ranunculus conform most readily to the concentric ring pattern, with never a petal out of line. The design becomes more varied and free-style if you introduce other flower shapes such as the bell shapes of lily-of-the-valley, ovoid clusters of grape hyacinth, the trumpet shapes of freesia, and many others.

When a posy is for a presentation or is to be carried by a bride or bridesmaid, you may prefer to adopt the professional method and replace all the natural stems by wires. This has two major advantages. First, it enables you to bend the false stems every which-way, thus ensuring the neatest of outlines; and second, it considerably reduces the weight and girth of the handle. Imagine a posy consisting of a dozen or so rosebuds, a couple of bunches of freesias, and a ring of ivy leaves, and you will see the gathering

A sheaf of marguerites and variegated lemon balm leaves make a refreshingly simple floral gift.

A cluster of pink azalea flowers and large variegated ivy leaves act as both focal points and camouflage in this dainty wedding pedestal arranged in a baking dish taped to the wooden stand.

of stems will be anything but dainty! The disadvantage, of course, is that once they are wired the flowers are cut off from a water supply and will rely on a cool temperature and frequent spraying to keep them fresh.

If you do decide to wire the flowers, it opens up more and more possibilities for the posy ingredients. You can, with a little time and patience, wire individual hyacinth or stephanotis florets; use the pretty trumpet shapes of alstroemeria (Peruvian lilies); or make little wired bunches of, say, pale pink or cream broom, or the soft pastel green and extremely pretty lady's mantle, *Alchemilla mollis*.

You will need medium-gauge stub wires, available in packets from florists, and a role of fine silver wire. For flowers with a rigid stem – roses and lilies, for instance – you can cut the stem about 2.5cm/1in below the flower calyx, place a stub wire against it, and wire the two together with the roll wire. Other flowers and florets are more easily mounted on false stems simply by pushing a stub wire through the calyx or base and into the centre of the flower.

Whenever the wire is likely to show, as it would in an 'open' posy design with space between the rings, the false stems, or at least the tops of them, should be bound with florists' tape known as gutta percha. You can buy this in rolls in a variety of colours, including white, cream, and green.

Once the posy is arranged, bind the cluster of wire stems together with raffia or roll wire, and then with a neat and attractive covering of overlapping ribbon. A pretty bow with trailing ribbons is a must, a characteristic finish to the design.

If your posy is for a romantic occasion or is designed to express a special sentiment, you could make it all the more meaningful by choosing flowers that convey a special message. In Victorian times practically every decorative plant was assigned a meaning, and shy young

suitors could, by the careful composition of a posy, express their innermost feelings without a word being spoken. You could, in this vein, include ivy for fidelity; forget-me-not, red pinks and red roses for true love; pansy for thoughts; rosemary for remembrance; and love-in-a-mist for, as its name suggests, perplexity. To say thank you in the language of flowers, you could include ox-eye daisies, which signify a token, white bellflower for gratitude, and fern for sincerity. To be sure that your message gets across, you might perhaps include a card conveying the flower meanings. This was especially advisable in Victorian times, when rival publishers produced dictionaries giving conflicting meanings of the various plants, with potentially disastrous results!

If your gift of flowers is for a wedding anniversary, it is especially pleasing to choose either floral materials or a container that is appropriate to the occasion. For a first wedding anniversary, designated the cotton anniversary, you could tie a posy with a huge, crisp cotton bow, or arrange flowers (in a hidden water holder) in a basket lined with pretty floral cotton. For year number five, wood, you might decide to make an arrangement in a square 'gypsy' or 'primrose' basket made of split hazel twigs – a lovely keepsake for someone who likes to arrange flowers herself. The 10th year, tin, prompts flower arrangements in a range of smart and shiny bakeware, or in an old biscuit or cocoa tin, complete with its faded advertisement. China signifies the 20th year, and is simple to carry out: a pottery basket with its criss-cross lattice work and dainty handle would be an attractive choice of container.

A silver wedding anniversary, the 25th, could be celebrated in style with a white arrangement in a silvered dish with two or three barley-sugar-twist silver candles and, for good measure, a silver ribbon bow. For the 30th anniversary, pearl, why not tie pearl beads around the neck of

YOU WILL NEED

- basket
- block of foam
- foil
- raffia ribbon
- stub wire (to attach ribbon)

- mahonia foliage
- tulips
- roses
- pinks
- sheep's parsley
- silver foliage

1 The pretty pink and blue basket suggests an easily portable gift for a christening. The foam block is partially wrapped in a piece of foil. The extent of the design is determined by the three sprays of mahonia leaves.

2 The tulips, roses and pinks are complementary in terms of colour and well-contrasted in terms of shape. The right-hand side of the basket is kept free of flowers.

3 As pretty as a picture. The finishing touches are the veil-like sprays of sheep's parsley and the exuberant bow of raffia paper ribbon (available from some florists).

CHRISTENING GIFT

a glass or china container, wind them around a basket handle, or thread them in and out of an openwork basket – a pretty touch for any occasion. The ruby anniversary, marking 40 years, prompts deep red glass vases or bowls and rich crimson flowers. This is the time to go to town with the deepest colours of dahlias, zinnias, anemones, lilies, and carnations. Remember that green is the most complementary colour to red, so the inclusion of green viburnum (arrowwood), tobacco plant, hellebores, or bells of Ireland, along with the foliage, would work visual wonders. The golden anniversary, signifying 50 years, sparks off ideas for a gold-and-white flower arrangement in, perhaps, a basket sprayed with ozone-friendly gold paint and tied with a generous parcel-ribbon bow. Or, for a really glamorous effect, you might even spray all or some of the natural materials with the metallic paint. Golden-sprayed roses look particularly attractive and will then be everlasting, a perfect keepsake.

It goes without saying that you will wrap or pack a gift arrangement carefully if it has to travel, but have you ever thought of making the gift-wrapping a part of the design? Choose a container with a regular cube, rectangular, or cylindrical shape – it might be a used food tin, a can, or a plastic box – and wrap it neatly, leaving the opening free, in the prettiest paper you can find. If it is emblazoned with a happy birthday, anniversary, Easter or Christmas message, so much the better. Arrange flowers to complement the now-colourful container, and tie it round and round with narrow parcel ribbon and a bow. It's an intriguing way of presenting a gift, and one that can turn an unpromising container into a stylish design.

FESTIVAL FLOWERS

Easter and Christmas are red-letter days in any flower arranger's calendar when, more than at any other time, we decorate our homes in celebration of the spring and winter festivals.

There is a particular joy to Easter flower arranging, when the gardens are burgeoning with colour, and flowers are more plentiful, and less expensive, in the shops. Popular spring flowers range in scale from the tiny, shy violets and primroses, perfect for display in eggshell vases (see the project in Chapter 2, pages 102 and 103), to the bright and showy daffodils and tulips. This is a time to be generous, to choose a large container – it could be a basket, a garden trug, a casserole, a wastepaper basket, even a presentable bucket – and fill it to overflowing with bunches and bunches of golden daffodils, a real impact-maker on a table by the window or in the fireplace.

Branches of catkins and pussywillow perfectly complement spring flowers and bring a taste of the country to designs in the home. Fill a tall, upright vase with the branches, and arrange daffodils or tulips to nestle among them. Arrange two or three shapely twigs in a pinholder on a shallow dish, and position daffodils or tulips to soften the outline. Or fix the twigs in a pinholder on a board or plate (they will not need a water source), and hang decorated eggshells from them. A cluster of washed pebbles, a handful of moss, or a spray or two of evergreen leaves would conceal the stem holder.

Decorated eggs combine well with twigs and flowers in designs for Easter, and introduce a craft that children can enjoy. To empty the shells, use a darning needle to prick a hole in each end of the egg and, holding the egg over a bowl, blow through one hole to release the egg.

A holly wreath or posy is a traditional design to hang on a door at Christmas. This one has the added textural contrast of frosty-green fir leaves.

Wash and dry the shells, then dye or paint them. Spatter-spraying with first one colour and then, when it is dry, another, gives an attractive mottled appearance.

You could display a collection of painted eggs in a layer of sphagnum moss in a basket, and bury a block of foil-wrapped foam among them. You might decorate a clutch of eggs in dark blue and red, and arrange the mixed and vibrant colours of anemones in the foam; or paint the eggs in traditional green and yellow, and arrange a handful of sweet-smelling pink, orange, and yellow wallflowers in their midst.

Bring the basket handle into the design by twining trails of ivy leaves around it, and include a leaf or two in the floral group to link the two elements. Or, for an extra-pretty touch, tape a small, foil-wrapped block of foam to the top or one side of the basket handle and arrange a few matching flowers and leaves to follow the curve.

Moss masking a pinholder, moss forming a simulated nest for decorated eggs – a bag of sphagnum moss (available from florists) goes a long way towards giving Easter designs a natural and seasonal look. You can use it to line a basket or any wide-necked container before inserting the foam, and use more to cover the stem-holding material before positioning the flowers. With its yellowy-green frondy and fibrous texture, it makes a sympathetic background for flowers, fruit, and eggs.

You can use moss to cover containers, too, so turning the most mundane household articles, such as plastic boxes and tubs, tins, shoe boxes, and the like, into sympathetic flower holders. To do this, simply paint the outside of the container with an all-purpose glue and press handfuls of moss on to it. When the whole container is covered, tie it around with a few strands of raffia, not only for extra security, but for appearance sake. Covered in soft and spiky moss, an erstwhile plastic box makes a look-alike nest, the perfect holder for a flourish of Easter blooms.

By contrast, and by centuries of tradition, Christmas is a time to deck our homes with evergreens, the plants once believed – because they alone kept their leaves – to have magical powers. A rope of evergreens and fir cones looped over a fireplace; a welcome ring on the door; a hoop of glossy and matt leaves around the base of the four Advent candles; a holly ball hanging in the hall; a mistletoe posy hanging romantically in a bedroom or decorating a gift parcel – there are numerous ways to bring evergreens into your Christmas celebrations.

If you have the chance to gather leaves for your designs, think beyond the holly and the ivy and try to include other evergreens with contrasting colours and textures. Cypress, which grows in colours as far apart as sharp lime-green and misty blue, juniper, mistletoe, bay, laurel (especially the variegated spotted variety), rosemary, yew, and off-cuts from the Christmas tree – mix and match the various types for the maximum effect.

One of the most versatile designs, practicable if you have access to a fair amount of evergreens, is a swag, also known as an evergreen ribbon or rope. You can loop one over the fireplace – keeping it well away from the reach of the flames – over an arch, a window or a doorway, along the banisters beside the staircase, or over a large mirror, picture, or wall panel.

To make a swag, measure a length of stout cord or rope, remembering to allow for generous loops and drapes, and mark the centre. Gather the evergreens together and cut them into short-stemmed lengths; about 10cm/4in is ideal. Bind the bunches with fine roll wire and then, starting

A simple design in a cup and saucer includes doronicum, kingcups, forget-me-nots and deadnettle. It is perfect for Easter morning.

2 Primroses, violas and forget-me-nots are added to the group, each species perfectly complementing and contrasting with its neighbour. This is a design that nimble-fingered children would love to copy.

1 Broken eggshells, washed and filled with water, make the prettiest of Eastertime vases to hold miniature flowers such as primulas and pulmonaria. Stand the vases in an egg carrier or a group of matching or contrasting egg cups.

YOU WILL NEED

- egg shells
- egg carrier or egg cups

- primroses
- violas
- forget-me-nots
- ivy
- primulas
- pulmonaria

3 Primrose and ivy leaves frame the tiny flowers in the third eggshell vase. Any one of these pretty vases, firmly set in marzipan or frosting, would make a delightful decoration for the centre of an Easter cake.

■ EASTER POSIES

at the centre and working towards one end, bind the bunches to the cord, the tip ends facing outwards. Reverse the bunches to work the second side, and cover the centre join with a specially prolific spray. Decorate the swag as you please, with false holly berries, fir cones, wired nuts, dried flowers, or baubles.

The pre-formed foam shapes that most florists sell are especially useful at Christmas time. You can use one of the plastic and foam rings – absorbent foam encased in a circular plastic trough – to make both a welcome ring for the door and a table decoration, including the traditional Advent ring. The method is similar for both types of decoration. Soak the ring until it is saturated. Position the candles, if you are using them. Cut the evergreens into short lengths, and arrange them around the ring, taking care to mask the dark green casing around both the outside and inside rims.

You can decorate a door ring with wired fir cones, nuts, false berries, rosehips, or baubles, and a generous ribbon bow. Tartan ribbon, in the Victorian tradition, looks especially festive. For a table design you can follow another Victorian custom and decorate the ring with bon-bons, fruits, or flowers. Brightly wrapped sweets, kumquats, tiny clementines, and glistening helichrysum flowers all lend a festive touch and add a dramatic texture contrast.

Absorbent foam balls, available in florists in sizes ranging from that of a tennis ball to a football, can be used to make hanging decorations and indoor 'trees'. To make a hanging ball, press a bent wire staple into the soaked sphere and hang it in a convenient place to work. Arrange short sprays of evergreens all around it; you can use just holly, just mistletoe, or a mixture of greenery, and decorate it with other more colourful materials as you wish.

To make an indoor tree, press the soaked sphere on to a twig or bamboo cane secured in a flower pot. Plaster of Paris is one of the most stabilizing of materials. Again, cover the ball with evergreens, clippings of silvery honesty, dried flowers, wired nuts – what you will. A pair of floor-standing trees decorated with evergreens and standing on either side of a door or archway has all the style and elegance of topiary bay trees; a small greenery and dried-flower tree tied just under the sphere with a ribbon bow makes a pretty and long-lasting table centrepiece.

Posies of greenery make lovely decorations all around the home. You can compose a sheaf of twigs and evergreens and tie them with a fullsome bow to take the place of a welcome ring on the front door; make a posy of mistletoe and dried rosebuds to hang over a bed; or make mini-posies to decorate gift parcels in an original and stylish way.

A breakfast tray in bed, a special treat for a visitor or on a birthday, is all the more welcome for a small nosegay of flowers.

1 The wire netting is held in place inside the rim of the pottery jelly mould with narrow bands of florists' tape. With blue perennial cornflowers on one side and golden gerberas on the other, the flower colours are well defined.

■ BANDS
OF COLOUR

2 Yellow roses and gold-flashed white irises build up the right-hand side of the design. Variegated periwinkle sprays, with their star-like flowers, complement the blue of the cornflowers.

3 The full-face pansies reinforce the 'blue' side and the strong bands of colour are separated by white sweet peas. The pink wild campion, so pretty among the yellow blooms, adds a touch of the countryside to this informal design.

CHAPTER FIVE

FLOWERS
FOR EVER

The prospect for dried flower arranging has never been brighter. There is an ever-increasing variety of colourful flowers and seedheads in the shops, all shapes and sizes of lovely blooms to serve as an almost everlasting reminder of country gardens in summer. And if you have access to a garden or the countryside yourself, you can gradually build up a collection of dried materials to use in flower arrangements all year long.

The openwork container gives a light and airy feel to the dried flower arrangement of pink and white larkspur, rosebuds and helichrysum. The stems are held in crumpled chicken-wire netting.

The techniques for preserving flowers, seedheads, and leaves are encouragingly simple: the principle method involves nothing more than hanging the materials in a warm, airy room. Store them in a dry place, position arrangements away from the full glare of sunlight, and the flowers should retain their charm and colour for years to come.

If you are gathering materials for drying or preserving, the stage of their development at which you harvest them, and even the time of day, is crucial. You need to capture most flowers just before they are fully opened. In the case of larkspur, for example – one of the prettiest of tall-stemmed flowers for dried arrangements – this means cutting them when some of the topmost florets are still in tight bud, and only the lowest ones are fully open. Everlasting flowers such as helichrysum and helipterum should be cut as soon as they start to dry on the plant, when they feel crisp and papery. Roses are a special case: snip them when the buds are only just beginning to unfurl.

Deciduous leaves to be preserved in glycerine should be cut in early summer, when the sap is still rising in the plant. Evergreen leaves can be harvested at almost any time of year, but avoid early spring, when the new young shoots are pale green and vulnerable.

It is important to cut all materials for preserving on a dry day, after the morning dew has dried and before the evening dew has settled. Midmorning and late afternoon are the best times. Plant material cut at high noon, when the sun is at its strongest, tends to wilt and lose its natural form.

Air drying is by far the most widely practised method of preserving, and one that is suitable for the widest range of materials. According to type, you hang the material in small bunches, place stems flat on a shelf or rack, or arrange them loosely to stand upright in a container. Whatever the method, put them in a dry, warm place that has a free circulation of air. An airing cupboard, the space over the boiler, or a dark corner in a well-heated room are all suitable locations.

To prepare the materials for drying, strip off the lower leaves, which would create unnecessary condensation in the drying room, and sort the material according to type.

Flowers suitable for hang-drying, either singly or in small bunches, include all the everlastings, such as statice, sea lavender, and helichrysum; those composed of a mass of small florets, such as larkspur, marjoram, lady's mantle (*Alchemilla mollis*), yarrow, mimosa, and golden rod; those composed of a mass of petals, such as cornflower, peony, zinnia, and rose; and a wide range of seedheads, including love-in-a-mist, poppy, lupin, mallow, and Chinese lantern.

Tie the bunches with a slip knot in raffia or fine twine, and hang them on a pole, a rack, on hooks or wire coathangers, whichever is most convenient. Check the bunches every couple of days and tighten the knots as the stems dry and shrink. The materials will take several days to dry; the exact timing will depend on their substance and moisture content and on the temperature and humidity of the drying area.

Some plants with a heavy head-to-stem ratio dry more successfully if they are placed flat on a rack (a slatted shelf in an airing cupboard is ideal), or on absorbent paper on a shelf or in a box. This category includes all grasses, dock, giant hogweed, and lavender, which is less inclined to shed its seeds this way than when dried by hanging.

A third category of plants dries most successfully by standing upright in a wide-necked container – wide-necked so the stems can fan out, allowing the warm, dry air to circulate freely around all the heads. Acanthus, gypsophila, bulrush, and hydrangea are among those plants best dried in this manner.

An alternative way to dry multi-petalled flowers such as cornflower, zinnia, and pearl everlasting and hydrangea, is by air and water drying. For this method, stand the stems in a container with a little water, and leave them undisturbed until it has evaporated. Then remove the stems, wipe them dry, and place them in an airing cupboard for a day or two to discourage the formation of mould.

A few plant types form a separate section within the upright drying category. These include sweetcorn, globe artichoke, carline thistle, protea, and garlic and onion seedheads, which need support just beneath the head. You can use the slats in an airing cupboard, or a piece of chicken wire stretched across a frame. Push the stalks through the holes so the heads rest on the surface, and leave them to dry for several days.

Some flowers are more successfully dried in desiccants, or drying agents. These include all flowers with an open, saucer-like shape, such as buttercup; trumpet and cone shapes; and multi-petalled composites of the daisy type (gerbera and marguerite, for example). For the drying agent you can use ground silica gel (you buy it in the form of blue crystals, and crush it with a rolling pin or in a pestle and mortar), household borax, sifted to remove any lumps, alum powder, and dry silver sand. While ground silica gel and, for the largest of flowers, silver sand can be used alone, both borax and alum are most effective when mixed in the proportion of three parts of the chemical to two parts sand.

The desiccant method of drying greatly extends the range of flowers you can preserve, and includes pansy, daffodil, narcissus, freesia, lily, ranunculus, anemone, camellia, and orchid. Some other flowers that may be air-dried give better results when preserved in this way, roses and peonies are examples.

To prepare flowers for desiccant drying, cut woody stems to within about 2.5cm/1in of the calyx, and cut off fleshy stems at the flower base. It is easier to mount the now stemless flowers on short lengths of wire at this stage, while they are still supple, than to leave it until they are dry and brittle. Push a short length of medium-gauge stub wire through the base and in to the flower or floret centre. Once they are dry, you can mount the short woody or wire stems on longer wires or thin split canes.

The method of desiccant drying is simple. Pour a 1.5cm/½in layer of the dry crystals or powder in to the base of an airtight tin or box, and place the flowerheads, arranged so they do not touch, on top. Then allow the desiccant to trickle slowly through your fingers or a paper cone on to the flowers, so that it comes into contact with every part of each petal. Use a spoon or brush to complete the cover-up job, then slowly trickle a thin layer of desiccant over the top. Cover the box and leave it undisturbed for at least two days; for large flowers such as double dahlias and chrysanthemums it's best to leave them for up to 10 days.

To test for readiness, use a small camel-hair brush to ease the desiccant away from the flowers. When dry, they should feel as crisp as tissue paper. Carefully remove the flowers from the container; at this stage, when all the moisture has been drawn from the petals, they are extremely brittle and can be easily damaged. Use the brush again to gently remove any residual particles of the desiccant that may be clinging to the petals.

Store the dried flowers between layers of tissues in a box or drawer in a dry room, or mount them on wire stems and store them, away from the light, with the wires pushed in to a block of dry foam.

Sift the desiccant to remove any plant particles, and spread it on a baking tray. Dry it in a low-temperature oven, then cool it and store in an airtight tin or jar. Some types of silica gel crystals are colour-indicated and turn pink as they absorb moisture; they revert to blue again once they are dried.

■ EVERLASTING PLEASURE

1 A plastic spike fixed to the base of the basket with a dab of florists' clay holds in place a piece cut from a block of dry foam. A fan shape of wheat ears commences the posy design.

2 Colour is added with short-cut stems of pink larkspur, one of the prettiest of dried flowers. Wheat stalks are inserted at the other end to give the illusion of a posy.

3 A handful of pink rosebuds completes the charming posy design, an arrangement that would make a delightful birthday or anniversary gift. The generous bow is made from a strip of raffia paper ribbon, cut to one-third of the original width.

YOU WILL NEED

▐ basket

▐ plastic prong

▐ florists' clay

▐ dry foam

▐ raffia ribbon

▐ stub wire (to attach ribbon)

▐ wheat

▐ dried larkspur

▐ dried rosebuds

PRESERVING IN GLYCERINE

Preserving foliage and bracts in a glycerine solution enables you to add a whole range of glossy materials to your dried collection. With their enhanced autumnal colours and glowing surfaces, such materials blend well with both fresh and dried flowers.

Use the technique on sprays of deciduous leaves such as copper beech, beech and oak; on evergreen leaves such as senecio, privet, ivy, laurel, eucalyptus, mahonia, magnolia, holly, and blackberry; and on heathers and the flower-like bracts of hydrangea and bells of Ireland, *Molucella laevis*.

Prepare plant material by removing the lower leaves and any damaged ones. Cut the base of the stems at a sharp angle to expose the maximum surface area to the preserving solution. Split or lightly hammer the ends of hardwood stems, and scrape away about 5cm/2in of the bark so they can more readily take up the fluid. Stand the stems in water for about two hours to condition them and give them a long drink.

Make a solution of four parts glycerine to six parts very hot water. Mix it well, and pour it in to deep containers to a depth of about 7.5cm/3in. Stand the stems in the solution, pushing them well down so the ends are completely immersed, and transfer the containers to a cool, dark place for several days. As the stems take up the solution, the water will evaporate and the glycerine will become absorbed by the leaves or bracts, leaving them supple and shiny. Check the material after about six days. It is ready once droplets of glycerine appear on the surface.

Wipe the leaves or bracts and stems dry with a clean cloth. Sieve the glycerine solution, and pour it in to an airtight jar for later use.

Large individual leaves such as laurel, magnolia, fig and *Fatsia japonica* may be preserved by total immersion in a half-and-half glycerine and hot water solution. When the leaves have darkened in colour and feel very pliable, remove them and wash in soapy water. Dry thoroughly, and store them between tissues. To mount the leaves on false wire stems, thread a stub wire in and out along the central vein.

The preserving process considerably darkens leaves and bracts, turning some chestnut brown, some deep beige, and others nearly black. You can bleach them by leaving the material on a sunny window-sill for several weeks, after which most leaves and bracts will have faded to a warm cream or deep parchment colour.

If colour is important to your collection, and especially if you long to capture all the vibrant shades of fallen leaves, you can do so by pressing them. Leaves dried by pressing will become brittle but, once they are threaded on wires, they can be used to spectacular effect in dried flower arrangements. What pressed leaves lack in suppleness, they make up for in their exciting variety of colour, from the fiery red of Virginia creeper to the soft gold of field maple, from the greeny yellow of chestnut to the bronzy yellow of the tulip tree, or whitewood.

ARRANGING DRIED FLOWERS

According to the scale of the foliage to be pressed, you can use a flower press, sheets of blotting paper slipped between the pages of a heavy book, or sheets of newspaper placed underneath a carpet. Fern and other 'cut' leaves give particularly pleasing results.

The art of arranging dried material differs slightly from the techniques used when arranging fresh flowers. In general, not only are the natural

Flowers and seedheads make an attractive decoration in a room corner as they hang in bunches to dry.

stems of dried and preserved materials a less than attractive feature, but many flowers are mounted on false stems, and so flowers are massed together in order to conceal them. That is why, in so many dried flower arrangements, the design appears to be 'all heads'. This does mean that, measure for measure, you will need rather more dried flowers than fresh to fill any given container – a chunky willow basket, for instance. But since dried flower designs will retain their looks for many months, and since the materials can be rearranged over and over again in other groupings, they more than repay the initial expense, time and effort that went into preserving them.

All the holding materials and tools you use for fresh flower arrangements will be useful when you arrange dried flowers, with only one exception. It is important to use the brown or grey, dry stem-holding foam made specially for dried flower arrangements. Like the green absorbent foam, this is available in small cylinders, brick-sized blocks, and a range of shapes. These include spheres of various sizes, cones, and rings. As the foam is used dry, the rings made for dried flower wreaths and circlets do not need an outer waterproof casing of plastic. Consequently, the finished designs can be much more delicate and dainty.

The main technique to learn when using dried flowers is the quick and easy way to mount materials on false stems. Once dried, both flowers and stems are brittle and easily breakable, and can all too easily part company. *Helichrysum bracteatum* flowers, the daisy-like everlastings sometimes known as strawflowers, are notorious for this trait. In fact, some florists sell the separated flowerheads loose, by the bagful, ready to be mounted on false stems. This is when medium-gauge stub wires become an essential part of your kit. To wire the dried flowerheads, push a wire through the calyx at the base and up through the flower centre. Bend a short hook in the top of the wire, then gradually draw the wire down through the flower until the hook is buried within it, and invisible.

Heavy flower heads such as dahlias and chrysanthemums can be mounted on split canes, which you can buy in bundles from florists or garden centres. If you did not do so before they were dried, mount the flowers first on a short length of medium-gauge or thick stub wire. Then place the cane against the short wire 'stem', and bind the two together securely with fine roll wire.

Bunching is another wiring technique that has many applications. You can cut snippings from large dried stems of, say, golden rod, form them into small posies, and bind them around one end of a stub wire. You can then use this small-scale material in designs for which the whole stem would be quite unsuitable. Try the technique with lime-green *Alchemilla mollis*, snow-white gypsophila, yarrow, achillea, mimosa, dock, astilbe, and rat's tail statice (*Limonium suworowii*); or, for an unusual effect, make up mixed bunches of two or more flower types.

Whenever false stems are likely to be seen in an arrangement, as they would be if you positioned them to slope outwards and down beneath the rim of a container, for example, they should be covered with gutta percha or florists' tape. The easy way to do this is to cut the tape to length, and wrap one end around the top of the false stem. Then spin the stem around in your hand so the tape covers it all the way down, slightly overlapping as it does so.

CHOOSING CONTAINERS

The great thing about choosing containers for dried flower designs is that there are no practical limitations: the container does not have to hold water, to be moistureproof, or even to be a vessel of any kind. You could arrange a cluster of dried flowers and preserved leaves held fast in a ball of florists' clay on a straw placemat or in the bowl of a wooden spoon; arrange a circlet of dried flowers around the brim of a straw hat, for a pretty wall decoration; or place them around the rim of a basket to be filled with fragrant pot pourri.

Shiny containers of all kinds have a special affinity with dried flowers. As they catch and reflect every shaft of sunlight and every flicker of candlelight, they compensate for the matt appearance of many dried materials. For, it has to be noted, most flowers do lose their characteristic sheen in the drying process, and it is only the everlastings such as helichrysum and acroclinium, silver honesty 'moons', and preserved leaves and bracts that present a high-gloss, light-reflecting surface.

Copper and brass utensils have a warm, cosy look especially effective with flowers in all the orange, bronze, and golden tones. A copper kettle with an arrangement of preserved oak leaves, coral statice, and orange dyer's saffron has all the glow of a fire on a winter's day; while a brass coal bucket filled with Chinese lanterns, sweetcorn, wheat, and yarrow makes a fiery arrangement for a hearth or a corner of a room.

Silver containers have a more sophisticated appeal, and look their best with pale pink flowers and silver leaves. In a silver mug, beaker, or tankard, what could be prettier than a display of sugar-almond-pink roses, pink larkspur, snippings of gypsophila, and frondy artemisia leaves? If there is a silver wedding on the horizon, consider making a dried flower arrangement as part of a gift. You may be able to find a silvered art-nouveau vase or a goblet that would be just right for the occasion. Take care not to scratch precious metal containers with the loose ends of crumpled chicken wire, however. If you do decide that it is the most suitable holding material for your design, protect the inside rim by taping all around it with a wide band of florists' adhesive tape or insulating tape.

Glass containers, too, have that extra 'glint' quality that flatters dried flowers, though you need to excercise a little ingenuity to mask the mass of dried stems that would mar an otherwise beautiful arrangement. One delightful way to transform a plain glass trough container is to place a piece of dry holding foam in the centre, leaving a gap all around, then fill this gap with colourful pot pourri, dry sphagnum moss, or silver lichen moss.

You can colour-match the pot pourri to the selection of flowers you will be using: a golden mix of yellow roses, marigold petals, and golden marjoram leaves teamed with dried flowers in those colours; a pink and blue fragrant mixture to tone with flowers in the red, blue, and mauve of anemone colours; and a nut-brown aromatic blend of spices and leaves to complement a countrified, autumnal arrangement of wheat, oats, and grasses.

The inter-meshed and shaggy texture of moss brings a new dimension both to a glass container and to the arrangement as a whole. For added impact in a rectangular container, slide pressed leaves between the moss and the glass, where they will be seen in colourful and dramatic outline.

With dry stem-holding foam concealed behind a high-profile camouflage, the glass container is ready to be arranged with a colourful mass of dried flowers. There's just one point worth noting: do not choose too many small-scale flowers to blend with a container of pot pourri, or the whole effect could look speckled and spotty. It is better to select medium-sized flowers, and a few well-defined shapes such as poppy or onion seedheads, to give the design clear focal points.

Ceramic containers may or may not be a happy choice for dried flower arrangements. Generally speaking, the more ornate the container, the less likely it is to complement the delicate tints and dainty shapes of a blend of dried flowers. It is a simple case of too much competition. If you do have a pretty and heavily-patterned piece of china, be it an old rose-

YOU WILL NEED

- rectangular glass container
- dry foam
- pot pourri
- plastic prongs
- florists' clay

- dried rosebuds
- dried lavender
- dried larkspur
- eucalyptus, preserved and bleached

2 Rosebuds and lavender, gathered into tiny bunches, form the basis of this charming countrified design in which the stems are all positioned vertically.

1 The rectangular glass container is fitted with pieces of dry foam, cut to leave a gap around each side. The space is filled in with a sprinkling of colourful and aromatic pot pourri.

■ FLOWER FRAGRANCE

3 Flashes of deep blue are provided by short-cut stems of larkspur and colour contrast by the sprays of preserved and bleached eucalyptus. This design would be suitable for a bedroom or guest room.

patterned teapot, a commemoration mug, or an urn-shaped vase, consider breaking with tradition and arranging it with a mass of dried flowers of one type. A couple of bunches of pink roses may be all that is needed to show off the teapot to best advantage; a bunch of white acroclinium in the ornate mug; and an armful of soft, fluffy white gypsophila in the urn. In the right container, a collection of dried flowers of all shapes and sizes has all the appeal of a well-stocked garden. Equally, in a different container, a mass of just one single flower type can look enchanting.

Earthenware and rough glazed pottery have just what it takes to show off dried flowers. And as the containers do not need to be moistureproof, you can use porous pots without the need for an inner liner. Flower pots make perfect containers. Arrange one with a posy of dried herbs for the kitchen – there may be purple sage, rosemary, and bay leaves blended with fennel seedheads and marjoram flowers – and another with a nosegay of colourful flowers in warm pink tones for the dining table. Larger flower pots, among the least expensive of floor-standing containers, are ideal for fireplace arrangements, and look particularly attractive with countrified blends of twigs, seedheads, preserved leaves, and large-scale materials such as achillea, tansy, and golden rod.

It is all a matter of personal preference, but baskets stake a strong claim to being the most sympathetic of containers for dried flowers. The textures and colour values seem just made for each other, and it is difficult to think of any other container type that looks more 'right'. You may already have several suitable baskets around the home: a shopping basket, an old picnic hamper, a lidded sewing box, a wastepaper basket, a high-handled basket once delivered with a fresh flower arrangement from the florists. Press whatever baskets you have into decorative service for designs around the home.

As with fresh flower arranging, your choice of holding material will depend on your vision of the finished design. If this is to be a fairly low arrangement of massed flower heads, you can use blocks of dry stem-holding foam cut to fit the container, or, if the basket is deep, placed on top of a 'ballast' of piled-up newspapers. At a low level and closely packed together, short-stemmed flowers will easily conceal the foam. For a taller or more upright design, crumpled chicken wire is more suitable and easier to conceal. If you are using a tall basket with heavy-headed dry materials, weight the container with one or two clean stones, so it will not be top heavy.

You can buy fashion baskets in an attractive range of colours, in just the sort of shades you can pick out in your choice of dried flowers. But coloured baskets tend to be expensive, and it is easy to spray-paint natural willow and other types for yourself. A shallow basket sprayed with a deep mauve paint looks dramatic with a cargo of peonies, pink larkspur, and purple marjoram flowers; while a pale blue basket looks fresh and bright arranged with lemon yellow and dark blue flowers – daffodils and delphinium, for instance.

Shallow baskets with or without a handle look especially pretty with a garden posy design, the flowers arranged with a handful of stems to look as if they had just been picked. To achieve simplicity and grace in a basket posy of this kind, you do need to employ a little artifice, as you can see in the project on pages 112 and 113.

Some of the prettiest designs are those you can compose on the dry foam shapes sold in most

A small posy of dried rosebuds, sea lavender and lime-green *Alchemilla mollis* (lady's mantle) decorates the back of a bedroom chair. It would look equally pretty on a door or over a dressing table.

121

florists. The circlets or rings, available in three sizes, make delightful wall and table decorations. Cut your dried material into short lengths – snippings from long stems and large arrangements can be used – and arrange them, packed tightly together, around the ring.

For a bedroom you may enjoy a blend of white sea lavender, snippings of pink larkspur with one or two florets on each, yellow rosebuds, and sprays of pale pink miniature roses. For a kitchen, what could be more appropriate than sprays of sage and purple sage, chive and marjoram flowers, and snippings of hydrangea bracts? And for a bathroom, you could blend sea lavender, statice, lavender flowers and helichrysums. Finish a wall decoration with a generous bow of satin ribbon, if you like to add a hint of gloss, or raffia paper ribbon.

The dry foam spheres can be used for the most delightful hanging decorations or – as with the absorbent foam ones – to make indoor trees. A dried flower ball of, say, pink and white acroclinium and snippings of dried leaves makes a charming design to hang over a dressing table, on a cupboard door handle, or over the back of a wooden chair. Closely packed with dried materials including tiny cones and nuts, the dry foam cones make pyramid-shaped trees, a very decorative imitation of classic topiary.

And then there are designs that need no container or preformed shape at all – posies.

Compose a dried flower posy or sheaf as you would with fresh flowers, and place it on a window-sill (though not a sunny one) or a shelf, on a dressing table or side table. Make a Victorian-style posy of dried cornflowers in pink, blue, and white, ringed around with silver leaves and circled by a paper doily, and stand it in a pretty glass container. Or make a free-style posy of, for example, dried broom, shiny everlastings, tiny rosebuds, and sprays of *Alchemilla mollis* and hang it on a chair, on the wall, over a bedhead, or on a curtain tie.

Whether they are arranged in a glass container or in the shape of a ball, in a basket or composed as a country-style posy, place all dried flower designs away from direct sunlight. Choose the wall beside a south-facing window in preference to the one opposite, a shady corner in preference to 'centre stage' in a sunlit room. That way the flowers should retain their original colour for many months, although they may eventually fade to a soft tint of their former hue. One further precaution: be sure to keep dried flower arrangements in a dry atmosphere in a well-ventilated room. Left to their own devices in a room full of condensation, they would reabsorb moisture and eventually develop mould.

Observe those two strictures – keep them away from strong natural light and in a dry room – and your dried flower arrangements are all set to give you lasting pleasure.

A small willow basket filled with dry foam holds a nosegay of dried flowers and seedheads including marjoram, yarrow, tansy and love-in-a-mist.

▌ GOLDEN WONDER

1 The bluish tinge of the split-cane bowl suggests an unusual colour scheme of watery blue preserved eucalyptus and sharp citrus yellow. The leaves are arranged first, to form a dome shape.

2 Pale lemon yellow helichrysum flowers contrast strikingly with the preserved leaves. Their twisted stems find their own level among the leaves. Small 'bunches' of florets cut from dried achillea are mounted on stub wires.

▬ YOU WILL NEED

▌ bowl

▌ wire-mesh netting

▌ stub wires

▌ eucalyptus, preserved

▌ dried helichrysum

▌ dried achillea

3 Flashes of even brighter yellow helichrysum and the bunches of achillea complete the simple yet effective design. The arrangement, with its hint of a refreshing aroma, would be especially suitable for a dining room or even a bathroom.

INDEX